THE HOLY SPIRIT'S WARNING SIGNS:
Avoid Life's Traffic Jams

"Wisdom is the principal thing; therefore get wisdom: and with all thy getting get understanding."

2024

Minister Sherri C. Kas, Sr

THE HOLY SPIRIT'S WARNING SIGNS:

Avoid Life's Traffic Jams

Are You Living A Toilet Stool Life?

SHERRIE C. ROSS

This book is dedicated to:

All those who have ears to hear and a mouth to tell others the Good News!

In loving Memory:

Dunn Lamar King; Misha DeAndre Howard; Clem Williams, Mable Williams, Willie Williams, Sam Williams; Clemmie Williams Hopkins; Mary Williams Holland; Jeanie Ruth Williams; Queen Victoria Joy; Ann Lawton; Joyce Ann Howard; Lucille Parker; Zeke Ross, Sr.; Vivian Newby Ross, Zeke Ross, Jr.; Dorothy Farmer; Theodore Cavendish May; Minerva Simmons-Milton May; Foster D. May; and Edward Lee May.

ACKNOWLEDGMENT

Special thanks to **Rodney Ross**, my children, and grandchildren.
Rick Chappell, Chappell Graphix; **Britney Scott**, Posh & Polished,
Author Jeanine P. May, Author SiJuan King,
Author Tiffany Bentley, and **Evangelist Esther V. Smith**
for your continued support and encouragement

CONTENTS

PREFACE

God is fed up with you, but His love is unconditional. His infinite patience for you has limits. You failed to heed His Word and disobeyed His commandments. You followed your own selfish desires, took idols, and worshiped them. Your state of mind is contrary to His Will for you, and you have not taken notice of the condition of your life. Sin has taken a prominent place in your daily activities. You wrap yourself in the pleasures and entanglements of this world. It is difficult for you to witness to others. You fornicate against God. You engage in ungodly intimate relationships and ignore God's Word, and you rob Him through your materialism, covetousness, organizations, and pride.

The Blame game is real. You need to point your fingers at someone and blame them, right? So, let's get it over with. It's Adam and his wife Eve's fault. God created Adam and Eve in His own image. They disobeyed God and ate from the forbidden tree of knowledge of good and evil. As a result, the first set of children they had Cain and Abel were equally loved, but they were distinctively different. Abel obeyed God and Cain had the opportunity to do the same, but like his parents, he disobeyed God. He hated his brother. In Cain's eyes, Abel was perfect.

1

the blessed favorite one. Cain was greedy or should we say slick and cheated God with his offerings. Now Adam and Eve's children are reaping havoc on the world.

We all descend from the same ancestors divided by color, race, ethnicity, and socio-economic status. This has caused emotional distress and harm to Adam and Eve's descendants who were mistreated, and enslaved by their brothers, sisters, cousins, aunts, uncles, grandparents, and friends. To witness the spectacle, we see today has resulted in injustice and sin. Proverbs 13:23 says, "An *unplowed field produces food for the poor, but injustice sweeps it away.*" This means it may also render Judgement injustice, and is the reason why some people are poor and remain so because they are victims of societies injustice.

In Luke 12:53-57, the scripture says, God did not come to give peace on earth. He came to bring division. Verse 53 Jesus says, *"The father shall be divided against the son, and the son against the father; the mother against the daughter, and the daughter against the mother; the mother-in-law against her daughter-in-law; and the daughter-in-law against her mother-in-law.*" And in verse 56 and 57 Jesus says, *""Ye hypocrites, ye can discern the face of the sky and of the earth; but how is it that ye do not discern this time? Yea, and why even of yourselves judge ye not what is right?*"

After reading these verses, you now have an option to "Bait and Switch" Maybe now you want to blame Jesus instead of Adam and Eve. Perhaps it flabbergasted you to know Jesus came to bring division. But before you fall swiftly down that rabbit hole, know this: Jesus coming, and His proclamation of the gospel intentionally brings division. Your faith in Christ makes you a believer and Christ intentionally separates you from the sinner and the world. When you go out and proclaim God's Word and His truth, this will bring opposition, division, and persecution. You must know people will not like your bible toting self. Your trying to live according to God's Word and His righteous standards will bring you ridicule and scorn. Peace and unity...Jesus the Christ the "Prince of Peace" came not to bring peace but the sword!

Jesus did not pray for organizational unity. He wants your commitment to abide in Him; your commitment and promise to love Him, your promise to separate yourself from the world your commitment and promise to receive and believe the truth of the Word of God; your commitment and promise to obey His Word; and your commitment, desire, and promise to bring salvation to the lost. When any of these elements are missing, the true unity Jesus prayed for cannot exist. [Zondervan The Full Life Study Bible KJV: note for John 17:21] You are called to keep your commitment and promise to remain in a relationship with the Father and the Son.

Zondervan's note eloquently breaks it down for those who are hardheaded and unconvinced that Jesus is "the Way, the truth, and the light" the note for John 17:21 says,

> *"To create an artificial unity by meetings, seminars, conferences, or complex organization can cause a betrayal of the very unity for which Jesus prayed. What Jesus had in mind is much more, than cosmetic 'unity meetings.' It is a spiritual unity of heart, purpose, mind, and will in those devoted to Christ, His Word, and holiness."*

Back to Adam and Eve's descendants causing havoc on the world. Why is it hard for Adam and Eve's descendants to comprehend they are relatives despite their anger and hatred for one another? Churchgoers, Synagogue goers, Mosque goers, and all the other goers around the world attend big prestigious buildings praying to God or sometimes a god, yet they discriminate against their brothers and sisters and expect to spend eternal life in heaven. Do they realize there is only one heaven? There is not a separate but equal heaven!

This squabbling discourse has caused humanity great harm. No one wants to be related to people who persecute and annihilate them but if you believe the Bible is the Word of God, then these are Adam and Eve's babies tearing up the world. That's You!

No Wonder history repeats itself because you haven't changed. You do the same thing repeatedly expecting different results. You ignored the reason Jesus came. You abandoned your commitment and promise to God. You abandoned your faith and the truth. You mislead the lost by your worldly views and activities and you cannot *judge what is right*.

If you feel stuck in life or feel you can't seem to break away from the same patterns and cycles? It is time for you to read this book: **The Holy Spirit's Warning Signs: Avoid Life's Traffic Jams.** It will help you recognize the Holy Spirit's warnings and keep you on the right path. What can you do to show God you truly regret the way you have treated Him and your fellow man? You can take a step back and evaluate your life in God's truth. Come to terms with your mistakes and attempt to right your wrongs. Speak up for God, tell others about His righteousness and His Word. Take a long hard look at yourself, your habits, and your busy schedules, and prioritize what is really important in your life.

No one knows when God's patience will run out. If you strive for true repentance and a life of righteousness, you can stand firm in your faith with the assurance God's mercy is everlasting.

This book will help you explore the way God uses everyday signs to warn you. Whether you are wrestling with personal struggles, relationship issues, problems at school, or problems at work, God's love, and desire to protect you is the same. You will learn about the many Biblical references that provide analogies to traffic warning signs you see. The author highlights the importance of reflecting on everyday occurrences and interpreting them as potential signs from God. These daily reminders can assist you in navigating through this life while avoiding as many traffic jams as possible.

We filled the book with practical advice on how to recognize and respond to the warnings the Holy Spirit gives you. It advises both believers and non-believers. The Holy Spirit's Warning Signs will ultimately open your eyes to see the incredible love and protection God has for you. It will also show you how you can live your life with purpose and intention. It's a powerful reminder to be aware of your surroundings and listen to God's warnings.

If you are stuck between a rock and a hard place and don't know which way to turn, the Holy Spirit's Warning Signs gives you the guidance you need. Your life can be a traffic jam. It can be so overwhelming and confusing to find your way without help and support. But what if you had help? What if you can recognize warning signs sent by The Holy Spirit to help you stay on the right track and avoid the gridlock? Read this entire book you will find answers. God's warning signs guide you away from the chaotic traffic jams in your life onto the path of harmony and peace.

One of the most important signs to be aware of is your conscience. When you feel comfortable with sinful situations or decisions, this should immediately alert you that there is potential danger or trouble down the road. Sometimes the Holy Spirit speaks to you through dreams visions and other people. You can receive warnings and insight about your current situation and your future. Pay close attention to your dreams and seek God's advice first and then advice of your trusted God-fearing mentors if needed.

When you take time to read God's word to find comfort, and encouragement, regarding various areas of your life, never ignore the warning signs of your conscience. Take a few moments each day to listen to your inner voice and discern what is right and wrong. If you pay attention to the warning signs sent by the Holy Spirit, it will be easier for you to avoid traffic jams and a toilet stool life. You will steer clear of people who don't care about you. You will stay on the right track and be sure decisions you make will be in line with God's perfect Will for your life. Followers of Christ know the importance of keeping their life in line with God's Will and trusting His guidance in every aspect. The Holy Spirit is the all-knowing source of wisdom and guidance. He will provide you with insight into situations to help you avoid making mistakes and getting stuck in the dreaded muck of a "traffic jam" toilet stool life.

But how can you learn to recognize these warning signs? It's critical to remember the Holy Spirit may speak softly and subtly. His warnings may not be as loud and obvious as you'd like them to be, but you can train yourself to pay attention to the quiet nudges and gentle signs He puts into your soul. Pay attention to how your body reacts in certain situations. It's not uncommon to experience physical reactions to messages or situations the Holy Spirit reveals to you. When you feel anxious in a certain situation, take the time to discern whether it's just you worrying or if it's a warning sign from God.

The Holy Spirit may speak through other people. When another person's words or actions stand out to you, pay attention. It may very well be the Holy Spirit speaking to you through that individual. Take the time to pray and ask for guidance. Ask the Holy Spirit for direction and clarity and be prepared for His answer.

If you don't hear God right away, don't be discouraged. Pray without ceasing, fast, and persistently observe the signs the Holy Spirit sends you. Prayer will help you discern the difference between your own thoughts and ideas, and the Will of God. Trust your decisions will be in line with God's perfect Will. No more traffic jams and toilet stool life. Share this power packed book with your family members, friends, and colleagues today!

PRELUDE

Are you living a toilet stool life?
Crap in and Crap Out?

When it comes to keeping your body healthy and clean, nothing is more important than the efficient removal of human waste. Toilet stools are a well-known type of plumbing system that helps to make this process easier for you. But like any other plumbing system, toilet stools may break down from time to time and an Out-of-Order sign gets posted. It is important to understand how toilet stools work, the consequences if they break, and how it compares to your own natural body plumbing system.

Toilet stools help you remove waste [deposited from your body] from your home efficiently. They comprise of a bowl, a tank, and a set of pipes that connect the tank to the sewer system. The bowl fills with water, which helps to flush the waste away. They are relatively low maintenance, but if something goes wrong, it can cause serious problems. When toilet stools break down, the consequences can be severe and potentially dangerous. If the water or waste does not flow out correctly, it can cause blockages in the pipes, leading to an overflow of waste—a cesspool.

A broken toilet stool can also cause serious water damage, or lead to a messy and unsanitary mess throughout your home. The toilet stool process is similar to how your body plumbing system operates. Your intestines[colon] move waste through your body, but if something goes wrong with your intestines, it can cause major health complications. Similarly, if something does not work properly with a toilet stool, it can cause hazardous conditions and health problems. Toilet stools are an important part of our plumbing systems by understanding this process and your body's plumbing system, you can protect your health and safety, and your home.

You expect toilet stools to work. Like you expect your body's plumbing system to work. When the toilet doesn't work, it's out of order. Are there noticeable signs when your body's plumbing system has failed? Symbolically speaking, you may live a toilet stool life. An out-of-order sign is a sign most people ignore unless it's attached to a toilet stool. A posted Out-Of-Order sign immediately warns you not to use it. Should you be wearing this sign? How do you recognize when your life is out-of-order? Can you carry out important work or tasks on behalf of your church, or organization when you are not functioning correctly or thinking clearly? Are you clueless about your status because of your chosen lifestyle? Does your barometer deceive you? Has self-indulgence in drugs, excessive drinking, gambling, and hanging out with the wrong people: rebels, devil worshipers, atheist, and negative social media influencer [whose platform entices or lures you into a sinful life] duped you? This is called a "toilet stool life." you are filled with "poop and crap" such as satanic influences: gambling, drugs, excessive use of alcohol, being confused about your sexual orientations, alternative lifestyles, and being spiritually lost. These are common indicators of a toilet stool lifestyle. This is a life of disarray, with no rules or expectations. It's a "party until you drop" mentality that leads to physical and mental exhaustion and harm.

So, how do you know when your life is out of order? It could be several things, including a lack of faith in Jesus; too much bible reading and no application to your life leading to boredom, disobedience, and an out-of-control attitude towards others, which can lead to physical and emotional harm. If your life is out of order, you need to bring it back into alignment with God's expectations. First, it's critical to reflect upon your priorities and how you spend your time. If you are spending too much time with negative or positive influences that pull you away from God, this is a problem it brings you down. It's crucial to create healthy boundaries and places of refuge to allow for your growth and development.

Second, it's important to make time for self-care and mental health. Mental health is a key part of maintaining a healthy lifestyle, it helps you recognize warning signs before it's too late. As stated earlier, if your plumbing system doesn't work and your stool of life is overflowing with crap that stays in your body with no place to go, then your plumbing system won't work [no wonder we see people walking around looking like a sour puss all the time]. They are out of order! This could be toxic and dangerous to your health. It is imperative that you take time to communicate with God, regularly. This reminds you of God's guidance and understanding.

Living a toilet stool life is a difficult, hard lesson, but it is possible to bring order back to your life if you choose to do so. With a conscious effort and dedication, you can live a God centered life of purpose and meaning. Sometimes in our lives when things seem way out of order, we feel whacked up, overwhelmed, confused, and lack the energy to press on. It's easy to become discouraged and feel as though the chaos will never end. It can be incredibly hard to get your life back in order.

You need to understand God's plan for your life. It is possible to make headway. It helps to start small. Priority setting is a great way to begin. Decide what is most important to you and focus on those tasks daily.

Eliminate the things pulling you off task[distractions] and restore order to your life. Time management is key. Allocate planned time for God first then slots for specific tasks, such as work, family, hobbies, and any other tasks you need to complete. You will stay on track and keep your life organized. With a timetable like this, you can easily see what needs to be done and when. It can also be helpful to create a daily routine. This helps you to stay on task and keeps you accountable for your actions. It may take a lot of work to get your life back in gear, but your efforts are well worth it. You will find you have more energy, more focus, and less stress. Plus, it will strengthen your relationship with God as you stay in tune with His plans for your life.

Let God bring your life back into balance. Dedicate yourself to achieving His purpose and living a meaningful life. So, this is where you might decide to throw this book across the room and say, "this is full of crap." You may even choose another four-letter word that begins with S and ends with T. You may think this person has no clue about what you are going through. She has no basis for these hifalutin words and can't comprehend what it's like to have your innocence taken by an esteemed priest, father, or friend, who raped you. She doesn't know "I am a victim." I am trying to chart my way through life without people judging me and throwing salt!

Maybe you are the person who says: "I am tired of everyone. Tired of people making me the scapegoat. Tired of being the person who has to fix everything for everybody. Tired of being the 'Yes' person. Tired of being the bigger person. Tired of being the unfortunate person everyone picks on and laughs at." Maybe you are angry with God because you feel God doesn't listen to you, and He has taken something valuable from you. Maybe you are tired of people making you feel bad about who you are, and you believe they devalue you.

Then someone out of nowhere, this Author, asks me the question: *Are you living a toilet stool life?* Trust me when I say pain whether it is self-inflicted or thrust upon you by someone else can send you in a downward spiral and cause you to suffer physically, emotionally, and mentally. So, It may seem like a silly question, but if you feel your life is out of order, it could be a sign of something deeper [like some examples that were just mentioned]. We all have an intrinsic desire to make sense of our own life and of the world. We want to be in control of our own lives. But when life feels chaotic and out of balance, it's hard to make sense of anything. It's easy to say when life throws you lemons, make lemonade. It is important to remember God is the ultimate source of peace and order in your life. He knows what is best for you and He will bring peace to the chaos no matter what your hurt, and pain may stem from. God wants you to find happiness in your life, and He will help you get there if you ask Him *So, keep reading.* The key is to dedicate yourself to living a life of meaning. If you focus on your purpose in life, it will stimulate you to take charge and bring the order to your life you crave. Spend time in prayer and ask God to show you where He wants you to go and what He wants you to do. Then take action. Look for opportunities to serve others God has directed you to serve. Serve with your time, energy, and talent unto the Lord. Serving others in need helps to bring order and structure back to your life when you volunteer and serve in God driven areas you are passionate about. Don't worship the volunteer effort and don't make your job or an organization God! Don't allow someone to use you and force you to serve where you feel dumped on or meaningless. You should hold nothing "Supreme" over God! When you are doing something meaningful, your life becomes more orderly and purposeful and prayerfully you will feel self-confident and unleash the power you have been harnessing inside for so long. Feel good about yourself. The word **"NO"** may become your new love language.

Finally, look at how other successful people [successful people based on God's standards] have accomplished their goals. How did they order their lives in order to succeed? Use knowledge to thrive. No matter how chaotic and disordered your life may feel, recognize God is in control. With God, you can live your best life! Take steps today to walk in the shoes of your purpose and enjoy your life.

CHAPTER 1

God Warns You

The Bible has many warnings from God about Satan's tricks. Throughout history, God has warned you against the devil's schemes. He walked you through Satan's wiles and intention to harm you. We provide you a detailed look at some instances where God warned you about the devil and what you can do to protect yourself from his schemes.

The author found the first instance of God warning you against the devil in the book of Genesis. In the 3rd chapter, God warned Adam and Eve of the devil's plot to pull them away from God. He warned them if they disobeyed Him, they would die. *"But of the fruit of the tree, which is in the midst of the garden, God hath said, Ye shall not eat of it, neither shall ye touch it, lest ye die."* [Genesis 3:3].

Adam and Eve made a self-destructing decision with consequences they never imagined. I am going to take the liberty to say they never imagined their son, Abel, would die at the hands of his brother, Cain. They never thought about their children progressing to a sinful nature to the point God wiped them completely off the face of the earth except Noah and his family. Look at Adam and Eve's children today fighting over land, principles, position, religious beliefs, and power.

Their offspring despise the skin color of their relatives. They find one another deplorable. We hypocritically say we don't judge one another but we do!

Another instance of God's warning is found in the book of Deuteronomy. In this book, God warned the Israelites to stay away from the devil's false prophets and idols. *"Ye shall not go after other gods, of the gods of the people which are round about you"* [Deuteronomy 6:14]. This warning makes you aware of the consequences of going against God and following the devil. Boy, do you run after the devil! You sit at his table regularly because you want to be famous, somebody! People don't have to do much to entice you or lure you into self-destruction since you want what they have. You alter your body's appearance to seek acceptance and approval even though God said:

> *"Let us make man in our own image, after our likeness, and let them have dominion over the fish of the sea and over the birds of the heavens and over the livestock and over all the earth and over every creeping thing that creeps on the earth. So, God created man in his own image, in the image of God he created him; male and female he created them."*

You are fearfully and wonderfully made [Psalm 139:14]. God did not mass produce you and he didn't take a cookie cutter approach to carve out your uniqueness. Your body is your "home" your "temple." You may invest in home improvement for the home you purchased and say, "why not invest in personal improvements of my spiritual home?" A little Botox here and a little there. You know how far man's investment can go for vanity. Despite God making you unique, you choose to look like someone else.

In the book of Job, God warns you against the severe consequences of falling into temptation. God tells you the devil is powerful and has the wherewithal to cause destruction and suffering if you follow his tempting words. *"For the thing which I greatly feared is come upon me, and that which I was afraid of is come unto me."* [Job 3:25].

Another warning is in the book of Psalms. Here, God warns you of the repercussions of giving in to the devil's ways. *"Let no man say when he is tempted, I am tempted of God: for God cannot be tempted with evil, neither tempteth he any man."* [James 1:13]. This warning lets you know God has a unique plan for your life, and you must be vigilant in fighting against the devil's strategies. This means you have to have your own God ordained strategy and plan.

The book of Revelation gives you a vivid description of the devil's plans for the end times and what your response should be. In this book, God reminds you to stand firm against the devil's temptations and to steadfastly follow God's laws. *"And they overcame him by the blood of the Lamb, and by the word of their testimony."* [Revelation 12:11]. God's warnings against the devil are clear and consistent. He often points out the dangers of giving in to temptation and the dire consequences of going against God. You must remember these warnings and be vigilant in fighting against the devil's tactics.

The Bible provides you with the strength and armor to stand against the devil to protect yourself from his snares. God is your Lord and Savior, and He wants you to be safe from harm. Throughout the Bible, God warns you to be on the lookout for the schemes of the devil and to make it clear to you ultimately, your battle is with him and not with your fellow man. You must understand your sole enemy is Satan. Satan is a liar. He will cause you to fight over small petty things. He likes to trick you by having you misinterpret peoples' intentions often resulting in misunderstandings and sometimes loss of life.

In Ephesians 6:11-13, you are told to put on the full armor of God, so you can stand against the devil's tricks: *"For your struggle is not against flesh and blood, but against the rulers, against the authorities, against the powers of this dark world and against the spiritual forces of evil in the heavenly realms. Therefore, put on the full armor of God, so when the day of evil comes, you may stand your ground."* You must be ready to stand your ground and fight fully equipped and ready. We are not talking about throwing sucker punches either.

This is a **F-I-G-H-T!**

The devil does not limit his schemes to the physical world, but also to the spiritual forces of evil in the heavenly realms. He is the adversary of God and man, and his beguiling temptations are ever-present. God warns you in 1 Peter 5:8 to, *"Be sober, be vigilant; because your adversary the devil walks about like a roaring lion, seeking whom he may devour."* To be on your guard against the devil's schemes, you must stand firm in your faith. You cannot be wishy washy or double minded. *"But when you ask, you must believe and not doubt, because the one who doubts is like a wave of the sea, blown and tossed by the wind. That person should not expect to receive anything from the Lord. Such a person is double-minded and unstable if they do"* [James 1:7-8].

You must be alert and aware of the devil's attempts to deceive you to compromise your beliefs. You must look to God for strength and not fall prey to the devil's alluring temptations. The Bible says, *"Submit yourselves, then, to God. Resist the devil, and he will flee from you"* [James 4:7, NIV]. God warns you against the devil for your own protection and benefit. He knows the vulnerabilities and weaknesses the devil can exploit in you, and He desires you to seek His help to avoid Satan's traps. When you are out there trying to do your own thing, your own way you leave yourself vulnerable to Satan. Satan knows how to suggest matters and circumstances to gain your approval. Satan will use you to lure your spouse, children, and friends away from Christ.

You must be cognizant of these warnings and be vigilant in the fight. With the strength and armor given to you, He equipped you to stand firm against the devil and protect yourself from his alluring temptation. God told you the devil is a powerful foe and one you should not take lightly. God knows this, and He has given you instructions how to protect yourself from the evil one as you will see in this book. God has provided you with physical warning signs you see every day to instruct you to put on the spiritual armor of God [Ephesians 6:10-18] so you can stand firm against the devil's temptation.

God provides you with His protective shield of faith [Ephesians 6:16] you are secure from the devil's strategies. God has given you the authority to cast down any argument the devil brings your way [2 Corinthians 10:4-5]. God said: always be *"strong in the Lord and in the strength of his might"* [Ephesians 6:10]. When you stand in God's strength and use the armor, He has given you, be confident your defense will be victorious.

God warns you with good reason that the devil is a cunning adversary. He knows how to make things look appealing and promises you pleasure, power, and fame, but it is only a trick to get you to fall into temptation.

He tries to cripple you with fear which is nothing more than False Evidence Appearing Real: FEAR! It is important you remember Satan's gifts come with a high price and are often fleeting. God wants you to focus on His eternal love, joy, and peace, which He has promised to all those who accept Him and follow His perfect Will.

The devil Is real and malicious, and God wants you to protect yourself from him. God's merciful warnings also remind you of His faithfulness and His love. By studying the Bible, using the spiritual armor God has provided you, and His protective shield of faith, you won't fall for the devil's game plan. God will never leave you, and heeding His warning keeps you safe from all harm. Don't think you will be victorious against Satan's plots by yourself. A battle plan without God is fruitless.

NOW THE DAILY WARNING SIGNALS FROM GOD THAT WE CAN GET FROM TRAFFIC SIGNS

CHAPTER 2

TEMPORARILY OUT OF ORDER

Being Temporarily out of order can be a problem when faced with complicated decisions. When Elijah challenged the Baal worshipers on Mount Carmel, he asked them how long they were going to be halted between two opinions. This is a good time to ask you this question. They were probably lukewarm with their decisions. With a double-minded person, they're likely to shift from one position to the next or speak out of both sides of their mouths. This could lead them to being scammed, conned, and deceived. Perhaps you have encountered a scammer or con artist in your lifetime. Maybe you have heard of the scams where you are told you won a million-dollar prize, but you need to send a check to pay the taxes before you get the million dollars you supposedly won. You may have even encountered a businessperson who did nothing but give you the Business!

Perhaps you met a person on an online dating site, and they scammed you out of money. Living a sinful life, such as fornication, adultery, gluttony, and boasting to name a few, leads to temporary alienation from God. It's impossible to serve two masters [being halted between two opinions]. Some people might disagree. They believe in Jesus. They go to church on Sunday, attend bible study and then do their "thang" on all the other days. They don't see any harm in that. They say: "I smoke my weed every day but Sunday. That's God's day." I kick it with my peeps every day except Sunday. I give God His day. This is nothing more than senseless double talk. From God's perspective, you are Temporarily out of Order. Temporarily because God gives you the opportunity to turn from your wicked ways and repent. He gives you the opportunity to ask for His forgiveness.

We've all experienced feeling temporarily out of order, wanting to serve God but also tempted to live in sin. It's natural to struggle when you face complex decisions, and you shouldn't beat yourself up over it. You should know the consequences that come with living a life of sin. God is clear. He said the wages of sin is death. You risk dying twice [eternal damnation]

If you stay committed to God and your faith, you will escape feeling temporarily out of order. The Bible calls you to make a decision and stand by it. If you choose to serve God, you must have faith and obey. You should fill your mind with nuggets of God's Word, find a strong Christian community, and pray for faith-filled opportunities to help shape your character and future. There's no shame in seeking advice and counsel from trusted friends, family, and pastors as long as their counsel aligns with God's Word. You have a bad habit of consulting with people who will tell you what you want to hear. People who will agree with you.

God warns you in Psalm 146:3 not to put our Trust in man. He said: *"Do not put your trust in princes, in human beings, who cannot save."* In Psalm 118:8-9 it says: "It is better to take refuge in the Lord than to trust in humans. It is better to take refuge in the Lord than to trust in princes."

Be honest about where you are and the struggles you face, only you can decide who you will call your master. Joshua 24:15 says: "…*but as for me and my house we will serve the Lord.*" Don't get stuck in a place of feeling temporarily out of order. Take steps of faith to serve God. Feeling Temporarily out of Order is a disheartening feeling. Whether it be from a career transition, a relational complication, or a setback in another area, feeling out of order is a universal experience.

Temporary means: "lasting for a limited period of time; not permanent." While it's hard to remember in these times, you must remember your life is ultimately in the hands of an all-caring God. While you can place trust and faith in everything from your own skills and abilities to the opinions of those around you, it's essential to recognize the higher power at work in your life and trust God over everyone else.

No single entity or power source other than God can offer you guarantees, it's comforting to remember God is with you in both the struggles and the successes. While sometimes you feel powerless, God never abandons you and He will always be ready to help you out. The best way to stay centered and balanced when you feel this way is to reinforce your relationship with God. Allowing God to fill your life can help provide clarity and direction amidst the chaos. Regularly engaging in prayer, meditation, and other spiritual forms of worship can help keep you grounded and give you the tools to manage the situation.

Don't forget whatever chaos and turmoil may come your way, God is still the ultimate judge and master of your life. Rather than feeling helpless and out of order, take charge and serve God in whatever capacity He leads you to serve. This means being kind to those in need, being honest with yourself about your spiritual convictions, and putting God's Will before your own. Remember that feeling temporarily out of order is a natural part of life. By placing your trust and faith in an all-caring and all-knowing God, He will direct your path.

Lean into strengthening your faith and take comfort in the knowledge God will never forsake you. When life throws you a curve ball and you are temporarily out of order, you may not know how to manage the disarray. In times such as these, remember to talk to God. Pray! God will never abandon you. He has equipped you with the tools to face any situation that comes your way. It is easy to become overwhelmed by your circumstances and to forget the power of faith and prayer.

Faith gives you the courage to move towards resolving your problems. Lean into whatever resources are available to you and take comfort in knowing if you put your trust in God, He got your back! There is always hope. No matter how bleak the situation may appear, your circumstances can change suddenly and for the better. By exercising patience, you can believe God will provide the means for you to make progress.

Backsliding–A Message of Grace and Hope We have all been there.

This Temporary out-of-order warning sign from God can also be a signal you are in a backslidden state. To back slide means to relapse into bad habits or ways. Believers, not perfect, will sometimes suffer a relapse and fall back into a life of sin. You may not be aware you have strayed from God's path, and it's hard to break out of the cycle of backsliding. The Bible provides you with several warnings about the danger of backsliding. In Proverbs 28:13 it says: *"He who covers his sins will not prosper, but whoever confesses and forsakes them will have mercy."* The Lord also exhorts you in Jeremiah 3:22 to *"Return, you are backsliding children, and I will heal your backsliding."* Unfortunately, it is all too easy to give in to temptations, and sometimes you don't realize you have fallen away from the Lord's path until you are deep in the backslidden state.

Thankfully, there is hope and grace available if you will humble yourself and turn back to God. 2 Chronicles 7:14, says, *"if My people who are called by My name will humble themselves, and pray and seek My face, and turn from their wicked ways, then I will hear from heaven, and will forgive their sin and heal their land."* This is a powerful promise from God. Confess your sins and turn away from them, and God will forgive and restore you. The book of Joel also has a hopeful message for the backslidden: *"Therefore also now, says the Lord, turn to Me with all your heart, with fasting, with weeping, and with mourning."* If you have truly fallen away from God, you should humbly turn to Him with contrition and repentance.

Backsliding may present one of the greatest challenges for you, but it doesn't have to be an insurmountable one. Through God's grace and mercy, you can come back to Him and receive forgiveness. You just need to humble yourself, confess your sins, and turn away from them. Then, you can look forward to God's restoration and reconciliation of your life.

Recovering from Backsliding: How to Return to God and Find Forgiveness

We all stumble and fall in our spiritual journey. Backsliding is a big hindrance to the progress of your spiritual walk. It is disappointing and demoralizing to have to start over again; however, with God's grace and mercy, you can always recover and keep going. Here are a few factors to help you recover from backsliding and return to God:1) Admit your wrongdoing and ask for forgiveness. When backsliding happens, you stray away from God and disobey His commandments. To recover from this, you must humble yourself and admit your mistakes. You must learn to accept what you have done wrong and sincerely seek God's forgiveness. 2) Repent and turn away from your sins. It is not enough to simply ask for forgiveness, but you must also turn away from your sins. You must commit to making better choices to bring you closer to God. Repentance is one of the most important elements in recovering from backsliding. Through repentance, you're able to see God's mercy and grace more clearly. 3) Renew your commitment to God: Abide in Him; commit and promise to love Him; commit and promise to separate yourself from the world; commit and promise to receive and believe the truth of the Word of God; commit and promise to obey His Word; desire, commit, and promise to bring salvation to the lost. Once you've asked for forgiveness and turned away from your sins, it is time to start new. Make a renewed commitment to God and His Word. Read the Bible and meditate on the Word of God. Remember, God will always be faithful and forgiving. 4) Receive God's restoration and reconciliation. Once you accept your faults and turn away from them, look forward to God's restoration and reconciliation. God is ready to restore all the broken pieces of your life. He is ready to bring back the joy and peace you were missing. Recovering from backsliding is a laborious process, but it is not impossible.

Understand when you carry guilt, you take on the guilt-ridden and conscience-stricken state of mind because of sin rather than seeking fellowship with God. [1 John 1:3] Adam and Eve hid from God. They ran not to Him but from Him. [Genesis 3:8-10] When you lack desire to fellowship with God, Christ, and the Holy Spirit, there is something wrong.

God's grace and mercy, always allows you to come back to Him and receive forgiveness. Just humble yourself, confess your sins, and turn away from them. [repetition on this point—hope it sinks in] Backsliding is a common experience for many who strive to be people of faith. It feels like you take a few steps forward, only to take a few steps back. But God's grace and mercy is bigger than your backsliding, to know how to recover from it. Prayer is how you show God you desire to be in an eternal relationship with Him.

In Psalm 27:8 David said: "*When you said, 'Seek my face,' my heart said to you, 'Your face, Lord, I will seek.*" Acknowledge God's presence in your life in everything you say and do. You want to live eternal life in heaven where you will praise and worship God eternally, but you want to escape duty here on earth. There is no escape He created you for this purpose. Restated humbly go to God and admit your mistakes. If you have done something you think is unforgiveable, remember God knows you will make mistakes, and His love and grace provide you with a way of repenting and turning away from your sins. After you humble yourself and confess your sins, turn away from them.

You must labor to stay true to the path of faith and embrace God's Will for your life, no matter how difficult it may seem. You can't go back to your old habits and lifestyles; instead, trust God and learn to live according to His teaching and commandments. I know this is easier said than done especially when the sins you engage in make you feel good and valued. You feel you are on top of the world. You feel invincible like no one can tell you anything. No one wants to be around people who have red flags with constant spoiler alerts. That's not cool. You want them to mind their own business. Do what they do. Do You!

I know you see those accountability jerks as haters. People who are jealous and just want to rain on your sin parade. "Not today" you say as you waddle deeper into the darkness of your sin. Remember the definition of backsliding is to relapse into bad ways or error. So, you kicked it with a married woman, man, friend, etcetera that's your business. Who is without sin, that can throw a stone in your direction? That's how a backslidden mind works. You know everybody wants to jump on people who commit adultery, fornicate, act jealous, greedy, and whatever else. But sin is sin! The consequence is the same—Death. Not speaking about blasphemy. We all know that's more serious. If you express these sentiments in a I am lost tone of voice than this warning sign, is evidence of you living a toilet stool life. Now that we have taken a slight detour and digressed just for a moment… there is redemption.

The last leap is to look forward to God's restoration and reconciliation of your life. God is faithful and will never leave you, even when you struggle. He will always forgive you when you humbly come to Him and strive to live faithfully. Look forward to a time of healing and being made whole again in God's grace and mercy. Move forward and look to God for forgiveness and restoration. With God's help, you will walk in faith and find strength in Him.

In the end, remember while you feel you are out of order, you are never totally helpless in any situation. You can always rely on the knowledge and tools God has given you to face any challenge that come your way. Trust God will never forsake you, and everything will eventually work out for the best. Romans 8:28 "*... And we know all things work together for good to them that love God, to them who are the called according to his purpose.*"

CHAPTER 3

It can be a frightening feeling when you see a warning sign saying, "Out of Order Do Not Enter." This is especially true when you are in a place, you thought was safe, such as a church or grocery store. Some of Adam and Eve's descendants feel safe in Casinos because they have the potential to be a source of great pleasure with delectable buffets, drinks, shows, and very often free tokens meant to entice you to play the slot machines and tables. Then there's the sex and orgies taking place in the hotel rooms. Prostitutes to entertainment depraved minds. You creep out abandoning your spouse to play games of chance. The atmosphere created by Satan is an optical illusion with grandeur and pomp and circumstance. You lie down with dogs, and you get up with flees. These places can also be dangerous, and it's important to heed the warnings of your inner voice when it tells you to stay away from an out-of-order place. When you enter an out-of-order place, you do so at our own risk. Even a place you expect to be safe, such as some nightclubs, workplaces, street activities, schools and churches can be out of order and a place you should not enter under certain circumstances.

Just in case you frowned upon the mention a church can be out of order, and you disagree know this, the bible has approximately 73 verses about corruption in the church. The bible speaks about false teachers in the church. We have made people aware about Priest, Bishops, and others who have sexually molested and or taken advantage of women, children, and older adults. There are people who disguise as pastors, bishops, gospel Artist, and other titled positions for fame, exploitation, and money. You must pray without ceasing and keep watch, so someone does not lead you astray.

It is critical to be aware of your surroundings and to pay attention to any warning signs that may be present. No one should ignore their inner warning signs. When you encounter a place, the Holy Spirit has marked "Out of Order Do Not Enter." You may suffer dire consequences if you enter a place marked out of order. You may encounter something not marked "out of order," but you hear God speaking to you about it. It's interesting how God's voice is clouded or fuzzy when you want to do something you know is wrong and you really don't want to hear God's opinion at the moment. Take this as a Reality check: you should not enter sexual relations with someone other than your spouse because it is a sin when you creep if you are married. Maybe God is warning you about a sexually transmitted disease the person has. Maybe the person is a stalker or murderer. Severe consequences may be an understatement if you get a life-threatening disease or lose your life. There may be long-term affects you may suffer if you take the risk. Pay attention to the warning signs and make sure you are not entering an Out-of-Order place, person, or thing.

It would be nice to have a warning sign to let you know certain places are out of order ahead of time. If a business or a home had a posted sign saying: "Out of Order Do Not Enter," it would be a beneficial safeguard of alerting innocent people not to enter. A warning sign like this could save many people from a great deal of hurt and trouble assuming they obey the sign. An out-of-order and do-not-enter sign placed between the legs of a person might be helpful too. Please understand, while a physical sign might not be present, your conscience is! Your inner voice works overtime to get you to steer clear of this pitfall.

Overall, it is important to be aware of your surroundings and to pay attention to any present warning signs. No matter where you are or what you're doing, pay attention and heed any warnings that appear. Whether it's a broken piece of machinery or a hazardous area, out-of-order signs are a serious warning and should not be taken lightly. Failing to heed an out-of-order sign can lead to serious injury.

Even an experienced adult with good intentions can cause serious injuries to people if they ignore out-of-order signs. Inattention to out-of-order signs can cause legal implications. Employees, for example, should always abide by out-of-order signs. If they choose to ignore the signs, they could face a lawsuit from a third-party. For example, if they deemed a machine out of order and an employee operates it anyway, then they could be responsible for any injuries that result. For these reasons, it is wise to think about your surroundings and to obey any out of order signs present. The the warning signs were posted for valid reasons. It's important to think before you act, and to take God's warning signs seriously.

CHAPTER 4

The stop sign is a directive to come to a complete stop, and consider what lies ahead. God placed stop signs in your life. Prompting you to stop and listen to Him so you can obey Him. If you are a parent, you can probably think of at least a dozen times you told your son to stop. He climbed on top of stuff, swung from the bedpost, jumped up and down and ignored your command until he hurt himself. Your admonishment may have sounded something like: "I told you to stop. I knew you were going to hurt yourself if you didn't stop." Or you may be the parent that responded: "See, I told you so." Despite your initial response, you kiss the booboo to make it feel better, give a gentle kiss, and send him on his merry way. Two seconds later you're hollering, "Stop! Get down from there! You are going to hurt yourself" as your child runs around the house without a fear or care in the world. Is this how you respond to God when He tells you to Stop?

Think about the time God stopped you in your tracks. You lied to your girlfriend. You told her you had to work and couldn't stop by her place. You snuck around with her sister and friends behind her back. God said stop! But your flesh burned with excitement of getting away with something. Adrenaline pulsated through your body, and you couldn't wait to get to your destination. You heard God, but you did your thang…not caring about anyone's feelings but your own until God stopped you in your tracks. Your car broke down! You got into a minor fender bender. You received an important phone call that caused you to return home. God clearly instructed you to stop, but you didn't. You ignored Him out of what? Fear? Complacency?

Arrogance? When you refuse to heed God's Word out of disobedience, you find yourself stuck in self-inflicted traffic jams drowning in your cesspool life.

It's hard to break away from your old habits and comfortable routines when God tells you to stop and take a new direction because you were having fun. God telling you to stop amid your youthful life is like using a monkey wrench to fix something that requires a screwdriver. Lately there's been a lot of conversation about The Greatest Generation; The Silent Generation; Baby Boomers; Generation X; Millennials Generation; Generation Z; and Generation Alpha. The conversations focus on the characteristics and attributes of people born in one generation. One generation is loyal while another only cares about themselves. Something mentioned solely to let scientist and researchers know God created them, they belong to Him, and all must bow down before him. God is the Alpha and Omega!

We do not retrofit the bible. It transcends all generations. When God says stop, He's talking to you not your label, title, or position in life. There is one body of Christ. You are a part of His body, right? You don't want to bow down, worship, praise, and obey, okay, good luck with that. As sure as you are living, you are going to die. Heaven or Hell will be your last resting place. Take your pick! God has kissed a lot of your boo boos along the way. He's picked you up and dusted you off. Like your parents who instruct you out of love and hope, God instructs you and guides you if you have the ears to hear Him. God said stop because He knows what is best for you. He knows when you obey, you will experience abundant life and find genuine joy. You don't have to bar hop to find you a man and you don't have to hangout in the streets to find the woman of your dreams.

Control freaks have a problem with possessing a little self-given power. They don't know what to do with the ability to manage others. They may be self-centered and lack self-esteem which is why they have to have their hands involved in everything. It is sad how they run behind people's back and stir up confusion so they can throw rocks and hide their hands. They prey on innocent people in the workplace and steal opportunities from deserving personnel because they want to promote their friends and their own personal agenda. They look for people they can step on or over to advance their careers or positions. Professed believers too. They have their backs turned so far from God until they don't know what hit them, until Cancer strikes, or some other life-threatening disease or disaster sends their hopes and dreams in a downward spiral. Fear replaced their arrogance and God became their latched-on friend in their time of trouble.

God, your Father, loves you and He will tell you to stop, and He will stop you! The next time you come to a stop sign, and you hear God telling you to turn around or flee from something, don't allow temptation to cause you to disobey. Instead, take a moment to listen and ask God about what He is telling you to do not your friend. He may tell you to stop and rest. He may tell you to go in a different direction. Either way, you must listen and obey. Take heed of God's Word and stop. When you stop you avoid the traffic jam of disobedience.

As stated earlier, God instructs you to stop before proceeding with certain decisions in certain circumstances. Just like a physical stop sign, God's Word has power and significance you should never overlook. God's Word guides you when you come to forks in the road on your journey. When you are unsure of where to go, or what to do next, your emotions and desires can lead you astray. God's Word reminds you to stop before you take action. His Word requires you to be still and think through your options before you make a decision. In doing so, you avoid getting caught up in situations that stress you out. For instance, if you face a decision to spend money on something you don't need versus something you need, and your inner voice says pay your rent or your mortgage, you need to Stop and listen to God. If you don't stop and listen, your wrong decision can make you homeless. It may leave you to beg people for money to help you pay your rent. Go fund me? The number of credit cards in your wallet with unimaginable credit limits are illusions to make you a debtor and not a creditor. The card is not magic. There is no Genie in the bottle to get you out of your credit card debts although bankruptcy may be your answer.

Maybe the decision you faced was whether to buy weed or food? Booze or food? Condoms or baby formula? Hair weave or food for the kids? Milk or popsicles? Your failure to make a full Stop to listen to God's answer will jam you up in a traffic jam of wrong decisions. Your plumbing system will clog up with bloating pains associated with stomach aches from your bad choices. Your toilet stool life will hinder your efforts and ability to drive straight into a life of joy and fulfillment. God's Word provides you with direction, perspective, and understanding when things appear uncertain.

God said stop giving dogs what is holy. He said stop throwing your pearls before pigs because they will trample them under their feet and turn to attack you. [Matthew 11:12] If you are a "do-gooder" you now know why there are some people who do not appreciate you and take advantage of you. They are pigs who will trample you and attack you every chance they get. You sow seeds into their organizations and various causes, and they don't say thank you. They use you! This happens when you keep going when God said STOP. Stop casting your pearls before swine.

Come to a complete stop before continuing, you will gain clarity and insight to move forward out of obedience to God. Think about God's faithfulness and trust His plan. His promises are true. He will never leave you as you seek to honor Him. The one thing you should not do is blame God for the consequences you suffer because you failed to obey. You pray and tell God you need food, God provides the money, but you spend it on something else. Perhaps you decided you would double your blessing by taking the money God gave you and gambling it away at the Casino. Then you curse God because He didn't help you win. You tell yourself that God should have given you the winning number. That God knew you wanted to double the money and he should have helped you. Of course, this is a self-inflicted traffic Jam.

In case you weren't aware, a traffic Jam is: "a line of road traffic at or near a standstill because of road construction, an accident, or heavy congestion. "When you see a stop sign, stop! Trust and honor God. He will lead you on the right road and provide you with the help and outcomes meant for you. Stop means Stop! It is a message to all drivers to obey the stop sign when approaching an intersection. Now and then you may feel the urge to speed up to get through a yellow light before it turns red. But when the light turns red, like the stop sign, you must always come to a complete stop-no matter what. This simple act of obedience is a reminder of the greater truth trusting in God and obeying His commands brings you to a life of clarity, direction, and purpose. When you approach a stop sign, you may not see what lies ahead.

The same is true for decisions, no matter how small they may seem. It is essential to always humble yourself before God, confess your sins, and ask for His direction in order to align yourself with His Will. Stop when God says stop. Obey the Holy Spirit's stop sign. Trust God, rather than yourself when you are unsure. Reflect on His Word, pray for His guidance, and lean into His promises rather than relying on your own wisdom.

The next time you come to a stop sign, remember it is not only a sign. You must physically stop. When you submit and trust in the Lord, He will lead you into a life of peace, joy, and fulfillment.

SOME UNDERSTANDABLE STOP SIGNS YOU SHOULD KNOW

*Stop Lying * Stop Stealing *Stop casting your pearls before swine * Stop excessive drinking * Stop committing adultery * Stop falling for the devil's tricks* Stop fornicating * Stop pretending to be someone or something that you are not * Stop bearing false witness against your neighbors *Stop mistreating people *Stop hoarding things * Stop taking vengeance in your own hands * Stop rolling your eyes* Stop gossiping *Stop being a nervous wreck * Stop worrying * Stop wasting your time on people, places, and things that don't mean you well * Stop being a glutton for punishment * Stop following people who don't have your concern or interest at heart * Stop being sneaky * Stop backbiting * Stop bragging and boasting about what you have * Stop spreading misinformation * Stop letting the devil use you * stop hating on people * Stop hurting other people * Stop being jealous about other people's accomplishments * Stop following the wrong people * Stop stealing other people's opportunities* Stop using God's name in vain *Stop putting other gods before God * Stop denying that Jesus is the Christ our Lord and Savior.

S-T-O-P!!!

CHAPTER 5

Stop Do Not Enter Inappropriate Relationships

We all know relationships can be hard, but what does God say about inappropriate relationships? You already know the answer: "**Stop Do Not Enter**." Recognize the warning signs in relationships that point towards an unhealthy dynamic. It is comforting to know God gives you guidance in the Bible on how to handle inappropriate relationships. Poor relationships can exist in family, business, and friendships. There are at least eight (8) bible verses warning you about terrible relationships: Proverbs 13:20 directs you to *walk with wise men and not enter companionship with fools because you will be destroyed*. Proverbs 14:7 instructs you to "*leave the presence of a fool, or you will not discern words of knowledge.*" Proverbs 12:18 instructs you stay away from a person who lashes out at people with their tongues…running their mouths uncontrollably. The verse says: "*There is one who speaks rashly like the thrusts of a sword, but the tongue of the wise brings healing.*" 1 Corinthians 6:18 warns you not to enter relationships of immorality. It says: *Flee immorality, Every other sin that a man commits is outside the body, but the immoral man sins against his own body.* God warns you yet again in 1 Corinthians 15:33 not to enter inappropriate relationships that may corrupt your morals. This verse says: "*Do not be deceived: Evil company corrupts good morals.*" Now you know why you sink and fall further and further away from God because you are hanging out with people who want to do nothing but live their life the Satan fun filled way.

God digs deeper into your heartbeat. He measures the pulse and the adrenaline moving to make it pulsate faster and faster. Here's a spoon of medicine to slow it down: 2 Corinthians 6:14, instructs you to stop entering relationships or partnerships with unbelievers. Here's what the verse says: "*Do not be bound with unbelievers; for what partnership have righteousness and lawlessness, or what fellowship has light with darkness?*" John 8:34 states: "*Unbelievers are slaves to sin*" and 1 Corinthians 7:22 "states that *Christians are slaves to God.*"

God does not approve of inappropriate relationships. He does not want you to be hurt by someone who is not honoring Him. Be wise and prayerful when entering relationships, and look to God for guidance on how to handle them. God places a high value on healthy relationships. He instructs you to avoid those who do not honor Him, and to seek His guidance before you enter relationships. God warns if you become deeply involved either by friendship or a romantic relationship with non-Christians, you head toward the biggest traffic jam of your life: turmoil and destruction…Constantly having to flush the toilet.

In Amos 3:3, God calls you out when you intentionally plan to engage in dangerous company. The verse says: *"Do two men walk together unless they have made an appointment."* Clarkes' Commentary on Amos 3:3 is:

"While ye loved and served me, I dwelt in you and walked among you. Now ye are become alienated from me, your nature and mine are totally opposite. I am holy, ye are unholy. We are no longer agreed, and can no longer walk together. I can no longer hold communion with you. I must cast you out."

God knows your plans before you make them. So, when you deliberately walk away from God to engage in the devil's wiles, you are on your own. God told you He can no longer hold communion with you. He must cast you out. The Stop-Do-Not- Enter warning sign serves a life-or-death sentence.

The Zondervan Full life Bible Study KJV commentary further explains this scripture. It states: "No *real fellowship can exist between two people unless they agree on fundamental truths. Thus, we can have no genuine relationship with God unless we accept His Word and agree with it. It is impossible to call yourself a believer and not believe God's Word."*

God says it is wrong to have a relationship with someone who practices idolatry, or someone who leads you away from Him. As examined earlier, God has some explicit instructions. He said do not become unequally yoked with unbelievers, and to avoid those who are not honoring Him [2 Corinthians 6:14]. He warns you not to change anyone, but to focus on your own walk with Him. God cautions you not to enter relationships based on anything other than His Word.

Seek His guidance when considering entering a relationship. He is eager to lead you and to give you wisdom in your relationships. You can rely on His Word and His Spirit to guide you in the decisions you make. He urges you to seek Him in prayer and to trust Him to give you the answers you need. You can rely on His Word to lead you and His Spirit to guide you. Ultimately, God wants you to find healthy and God-honoring relationships. This brings glory to His name. Considering these scripture highlights, it is safe to say for right relationships, God must be in control at the center of your life. God knows what is best for you. Your flesh may want to go in a different direction but when God says "Stop! Do not enter," Be warned for your own good. When you ignore God, you do so at our own peril.

God may warn you as a feeling or thought. You may sense something is wrong, and it's best to avoid the situation, but if you push forward anyway, you maybe headed for unwelcomed consequences. This is true of sin. If you enter a situation against God's will, beware there may likely be severe punishment more than what you bargained for. To avoid sin, you must have a strong relationship with God. Reverence God and have a constant dialogue with Him. Trust God to give you warnings about right and wrong relationships. He wants you to be safe. If He told you not to enter a situation, **"Stop! Do not enter."**

Kids get upset with their parents sometimes because they think their parents are overprotective and don't respect their boundaries. Some of them think their parents' baby them and want them to follow in their footsteps. They don't want to be like their parents, and they don't want their parents in their business. But like God, parents have rules and expectations. No one wants to see their kids hang out with the wrong crowd, going to the wrong places, and not heeding parental warnings. Usually, the parents are right, and the kids end up suffering consequences for their actions. When you obey your parents, God will help you stay away from sin and its deadly ramifications.

Some parents have very busy schedules and sometimes no time for their children. TikTok, Instagram, Facebook, and other social media platforms along with Roblox, Fortnite, Mario super brothers, grand theft auto, and other games entertain children and occupy space, time, and opportunity, their absent parents should have. God is not like your parents in this respect. He is never too busy for his children. He expects children will grow to love, honor, and worship Him. It is not God's desire for you to fill your children's minds with entertainment and games that point them away from God and the purpose He has for their life. Turn your television off if it teaches the wrong values and message to your children.

For the grown folks who want to morph people into something they are not: Stop asking God to make Billy over so you can enter a fornicating relationship with him or her. Especially when God has thrown all kinds of red flags at you. Stop lying and telling people you asked God, and he told you it was okay to sleep with Billy because you are going to get married soon. Hello, the bible assures you God would not counsel you to do something that conflicts with his Word. The Word says, *"It's better to marry than to burn."* Don't ask God if you should tell a "little white lie" so you can get the opportunity you want or the upper hand over someone.

In 1 Corinthians 7-9 Apostle Paul says: *"I wish all men were as I am. But each man has his own gift from God: one has this gift, another that. Now to the unmarried and the widows I say: It is good for them to stay unmarried, as I am. But if they cannot control themselves, they should* marry, for it is better to marry than to burn with passion." Meaning if you cannot stop groping on one another, having sexual intercourse, and whatever else you put your lustful minds to, it's better for you to get married. Why? Because sex outside of marriage is fornication and fornication is a sin against your body.

In relationships, listen to the Holy Spirit. If they tempt you to ignore God's voice because the relationship is attractive and brings you pleasure, then you are making a wrong choice and will surely suffer the consequences for your disobedience. Sometimes, your inner voice warns you to stay away, that's why it's important to know when God is saying: **"STOP DO NOT ENTER."**

God's wisdom is beneficial to you, and He cares about your relationships, so listen to Him when He cautions you to stay away from certain people. Doing so keeps you from sin and negative consequences. We all have different relationships and God will give you different warnings about them. You will make mistakes, but taking action based on God's guidance will help you avoid serious consequences. When you receive the warning "STOP-DO NOT ENTER," take time to consider why God is warning you. Once you understand the reason behind the warning, it will be easier to know how to handle the situation.

Knowledge of God's Word can help you discern the warning accurately. Sometimes, you continue in a relationship that God has warned you against. It's hard to leave something that brings you pleasure or joy or and it's attractive. You may be hesitant to believe God knows what is best for you, or you may deny a relationship is unhealthy. Remember, God's wisdom is perfect, and He cares about your relationships. When He warns you to stay away from someone, listen and heed the warning and take action. Doing so will help you stay away from sin and potential hardships, while helping you to live in obedience to God's perfect wisdom.

You face temptation in life, and God has given you a simple command. Obedience is required to live a life under His Will. Strive to obey God's instructions. It will free you from guilt and give you relief from the bad choices you may have made.

Satan never tells you the truth or the entire story when he tempts you to sin. His slippery tongue says the things you want to hear including false statements about a person's feelings about you. He will not say Billy really don't like you he's just trying to get in your pants. Honest real talk will never come from his lips unless there is some sort of bonus, he gets out of it. Like more sin!

God also speaks about how you should treat each other in relationships. He says you should not be jealous, but you should love one another as God loves you. He says we should honor and respect each other, and in Ephesians 5:33 He says, *"Each one of you must love his wife as himself, and let the wife see she respects her husband."*

God's Word gives you valuable instruction on how to walk through tough relationships. In Matthew 18:15-17, Jesus says, "If your brother or sister sins against you, point out their fault, just between the two of you. If they listen to you, you have won them over. But if they will not listen, take one or two others along, so every matter may be established by the testimony of two or three witnesses." Though this passage was written to deal with conflict between two believers, the principles can still apply to learning how to handle tough relationships. You can take these words of Jesus and rely on them as you seek to reconcile with your brothers and sisters in Christ.

God also tells you to forgive, even if it's difficult to do so. In Mark 11:25 Jesus teaches you, *"And when you stand praying, if you hold anything against anyone, forgive them, so that your Father in heaven may forgive you your sins."* We all struggle to forgive, but it's an essential part of any healthy relationship. We all are imperfect, and we all need grace and mercy from one another and from God.

I must admit, avoiding temptation is not a picnic in the park, and it is natural to be drawn to it. Successful avoidance of sin is to practice self-control and discipline. When you find yourself tempted to do something against God's commands, you must have the mental strength to **STOP DO NO ENTER** and choose the path of obedience instead. God's commands are for your benefit and obedience leads to a healthier, happier life. Listen heed God's warning: STOP DO NOT ENTER. Avoid sin and its consequences while living a life of obedience according to God's perfect plan.

CHAPTER 6

Stop Here for Jesus

Have you ever seen a sign saying, "Stop Here For Jesus"? Not until now. Though it may seem small, this sign holds a powerful admonition to take the time to slow down and give thanks to God. Life can get very stressful and busy, and you can forget to pause and stop for Jesus. Stopping to spend time with Jesus, whether it's through prayer or worship, will help calm your mind and bring you closer to Him. When you stop and spend time with Jesus, He encourages you to be the person He wants you to be, kind, caring, faithful, and loving. You can open your heart and mind to God's transformative power and show your faith and trust you have in Him. Be humbled and comforted in knowing He loves you and wants nothing more than your happiness.

When you feel overwhelmed with anxiety, depressed, or exhausted, look for the stop sign that reminds you to Stop Here for Jesus. There is mental health healing Power in God's Word. You miss out because you don't read the Bible or pray to God for wisdom and understanding. Who better to get answers from, than the one who created you and knows everything about you? Take intentional steps to pause and be in the presence of God and His mercy and grace. Think about the strength He provides to help you through life's hardships and tribulations. Not just petty things but real humongous stuff. His infinite love surrounds you so enjoy the peace that comes with it. Stop Here for Jesus. Let this sign entice you to make Jesus first, and incorporate God into your daily life and spend quality time with Him. Give thanks for His grace and mercy and allow Him to work in you.

God's love is powerful and is certainly something to stop and thank Him for. Offer Gratitude. Don't stay caught up in the hustle and bustle of day-to-day life. Stop rushing from one task to the next without taking time to pause and spend quality time with Jesus. Too often, your moments of refreshment and peace are pushed aside for something else. I am certain you can think of an entire laundry list of things that pop up all the time. That's why it's imperative to stop and focus on Jesus.

There is so much chaos going on in the world right now. It appears like people have lost their minds and their way. All kinds of out of the ordinary things are happening. The position of the United States of America. its Presidential woes and clutters of retaliations of all sorts. Litigations and investigations high interest rates, food, and gas prices. Faced with struggling families and homelessness. These are concrete reasons it is necessary to have a one-on-one relationship with God. You should want to know God intimately to feel comfortable talking to Him about everything. You can't go wrong with having an intimate relationship with God, why not? You do so with everyone else.

Maybe you don't know how to pause, and you don't know how to seek God's face. Give thanks for His grace and mercy and allow Him to work in you. When you pause, take a deep breath, and enter His presence. Take a few moments to release all of your worries, cares, and stress, lay them down at His feet, and just rest in Him and enjoy His presence.

Stop here for Jesus. Be amazed, at the power of His love. His love is unconditional. It is a power so great no one can deny it. His love is strong and unyielding. His love is gentle, patient, kind, and forgiving. Thank Him for His love no man can match. Stop here for Jesus offer thanksgiving for all He has done in your life. Thank Him for how He has blessed you, providing strength and comfort in times of difficulty. Reflect on how He has been with you, always guiding you, providing love and protection. Thank Him for the peace and joy He brings into your life. Thank him for the blood donor, the organ donor, the person who donated bone marrow, thank Him for chemotherapy, and radiation that saved and prolonged your life. Thank him for the job you have and the resources you gain from it. Stay connected to the vine because Jesus is your lifeline.

Take a few moments to bow down and pray to Jesus. Show Him your appreciation and gratitude and give Him time to work in your life. His love is powerful, and this is certainly something to stop and thank Him for. When you take the time to pause, spend time with Him, and offer Him sincere gratitude, His presence will overwhelm you with love. God even helps you with your schoolwork if you ask. He can make both the questions and answers plain to you. He will spiritually take the test for you of course through you. Sometimes in my profession I didn't know the answer to something but as good as God is, he would show me where to find the answers as well as how to win my client's case. There is nothing God can't do for those who trust and believe Him.

Stop Here for Jesus, ask Jesus what your purpose is. Ask him to reveal it to you and make it plain. Learn what steps you can take to prepare for God's answer. Position yourself to be in "ready" mode all the time. Guard your heart and open your mind for what God will have you to do. Know you are unique. What God has for you is for you! He doesn't take the cookie cutter approach, nor does He apply a one size fits all approach. You are valuable to God and all the people whose lives you will be a part of throughout your life.

If you are one of God's overwhelmed children, who feels the demand of life is taking a toll on you, prayer will turn your life around. You might be overwhelmed because you try to do everything yourself. You are tired of telling people what to do, tired of cleaning up after people; tired of people dropping off their kids, pets, and significant others at your doorstep; tired of siblings who don't help with the care of your parents, and they sparingly visit or call. The list of things you grow tired of will only increase and add to your stress if you don't stop at the knee of Jesus and ask him to help you.

It can be too easy to get lost in your complicated life; complicated lifestyles; complicated situations and circumstances. Thankfully, there is a way to pause and give thanks for all the blessings in your life—Stop Here for Jesus. This is an invitation to pause and reflect on how much Jesus loves you. Ponder on all He has done and will do for you. No matter how hard life may get, unlike your doctors, teachers, bishops, mental health therapist, Jesus never leaves your side. He is always there, ready to give you rest and peace during everything going on in your life. Praise Him for the goodness and love He has given you throughout your life. Tell Him how He has blessed you and affected your life! Don't take God for granted.

You may be torn up from the floor up. It doesn't matter God got you. Crack cocaine, heroin, fentanyl, and other drugs don't have to possess and conquer you. You were created to win. **YOU ARE A WINNER!** Stop, all the stress and strife in your life by giving it all to Jesus. 1 Peter 5:7 says: *"casting all your cares [all of your anxieties, all your worries, and all of your concerns, once and for all] on Him, for he cares about you [with deepest affection, and watches over you carefully]."* Give thanks to God who gives you true peace.

At the knee of Jesus, we learn:

The Bible teaches God does not condone hatred and has even commanded us to love one another [John 13:34]. Jesus himself said, *"By this everyone will know that you are my disciples, if you love one another"* [John 13:35]. He also said, *"Love your enemies"* [Matthew 5:44]. We are called to be peacemakers and to pursue peace and reconciliation [Matthew 5:9]. The Bible says that all people have sinned and fall short of the glory of God [Romans 3:23]. No one is perfect, and this includes all descendants of Adam and Eve's family.

We are not called to judge each other, but to show compassion and mercy. We are called to forgive and seek to reconcile with those who have wronged us. Jesus said, "Forgive, and you will be forgiven" (Luke 6:37). God desires for people to live in peace and unity. We have hope this will one day be a reality through the salvation of Jesus Christ.

Believers primary concern should be to lead others to the Lord, and to pray for their spiritual growth and protection. We are all part of the same family, and all of humanity needs a Savior. We can work together to bring about peace and unity in the world.

We can start by building relationships and showing understanding and love towards one another. We can come together and celebrate the common thread which is the love of God for all of Adam and Eve's children. No matter what color, race, ethnicity, or culture, God loves and cares for us all. Let us open our hearts and minds to fully understand the power of love and forgiveness. Strive to bring about a world filled with love and understanding. Let us remember Jesus came to save us all.

No matter how divided the world may be, Adam and Eve's descendants can live in peace, love, and unity. God has given you the gift of free will, and it is up to you to decide how to use it. We each have the power to make a difference in our world. We can choose to leave behind hatred, anger, and animosity and choose instead to embrace love, understanding, and unity. Together, we can all do our part to bring healing and peace to our world. Let us turn our hearts towards each other and strive for unity and harmony. Let us come together and honor the bond of family among Adam and Eve's children by cherishing the love God has given us. By loving, understanding, and forgiving one another, we can make a world where Adam and Eve's children can live in peace.

Adam and Eve's descendants fought and argued over trivial matters, and it seems no matter what either side said, it would never be enough to bring about peace. As their descendants, we must strive to be better than this and create a bond of understanding and love between us. When Adam and Eve's children fight, remember we are all part of the same family, and such disputes can be harmful to relationships and cause tension and animosity. We must learn from the mistakes of our ancestors and reach out with open arms and be willing to listen to all perspectives. We should try to understand each other's unique perspective and search for common ground to build bridges of communication.

You can also try to focus on the positive and allow love and acceptance to trump negative thoughts. Be mindful not to get angry at each other's differences and focus on finding solutions that work for everyone. We must remember even though we are all part of the same family, we have different opinions and outlooks. We should take time to listen and be understanding, even if we disagree. A positive approach to bring peace and harmony among Adam and Eve's children is daunting. You should use your God-given gifts to bring about understanding and compassion. Remember to pray for their spiritual growth and protection. We can work together to bring about peace and unity in the world.

The story of Adam and Eve's children fighting is a powerful reminder of the importance of prayer and unity in our world today. As the first family, Adam and Eve experienced firsthand the struggles of siblings squabbling and fighting despite being part of the same loving family. Despite their differences, they still showed a spirit of understanding and willingness to forgive. This is a lesson for you today as well

In order for you to bring peace and unity in the world today, you need to remember to pray for each other's spiritual growth and protection. Praying as part of a family and for each other brings, about profound changes and healing in your life. The power of prayer is something you cannot underestimate, and it can be a powerful tool for making a difference in the world. You must also remember you need a Savior.

Regardless of your faith or beliefs, we all need to be saved from sin and from ourselves. Therefore, it is important for us to come together in prayer, love, and understanding. We do not have to agree on everything, but we can still respect each other and come together to show love and compassion for one another.

When you Stop and spend time with Jesus, you will find yourself with renewed strength and joy. Jesus will fill you with a peace beyond all understanding. You will come away knowing you are deeply and unconditionally loved and cherished by the King of Kings. Take a break and **Stop Here for Jesus.** Get a grip on how much He loves you. Worship and praise him without ceasing for the amazing things He has done for you. His presence and love will bless you.

CHAPTER 7

Do Not Enter Wrong Way-Navigating Life With God's Guidance

You know the feeling of fear that comes when you see the 'Do Not Enter Wrong Way' sign while you are driving the wrong way: Faced with making a swift course correction to save yourself from a deadly mistake. But what about the signs God placed in the Scriptures to warn you when you're going on the wrong path and headed in the wrong direction? God has made it clear if you don't choose to serve Him, you chose Satan. It's essential to recognize the warning signs God placed in the Bible.

You should take the time to reflect on your actions and ask yourself if you are doing what God wants you to do. Are you entering relationships, partnerships, and friendships that align with God's will or are you continuing on the wrong path? Think about how you fix things, speak to people, treat people. Think about how you walk and run through life doing things you should not be doing. Pray to stay on the right course. In moments of confusion or doubt, remember to turn to God for guidance. Only with God can you be sure you're doing things the right way. The next time you come across a 'Do Not Enter Wrong Way' sign, obey it and remember God has placed the same signposts on your journey through life. Heed His warnings, and stay the course.

No one relishes the feeling of being in the wrong place at the wrong time. But this wrong way sign can also serve as a lesson for your daily life. Recently, an inebriated driver went up the ramp on I-75 the wrong way. That driver had a head on collision with a vehicle. The drunk driver lost his life. The driver hit by the drunk driver suffered minor injuries. In the blink of an eye, you can find yourself in troubling situations you feel you can't get out of. Whether it be financial trouble, depression, or a broken relationship, the wrong way sign is a signal you need to make a change.

The change might be scary, and it is not something fixed overnight. This is not something you should do by yourself. Remember, stop, and spend time with Jesus. Ask Him to order your footsteps and point you in the right direction. You will need to put in the hard work, and with God's help, you can make those changes. God has the best plans for you, and He will never steer you in the wrong direction. The "Do Not Enter-Wrong Way" sign directs you to keep an open ear for His warnings.

God's warning will come in many forms, whether it be a teacher, boss, friend, or a scripture. Do not be afraid to act on these warnings and get off the wrong path. The wrong way sign lets you know you need to put things into perspective. You cannot rely on your own judgement and should always seek God's guidance. As you encounter the dreaded "Do Not Enter Wrong Way" sign, always obey it and heed its warnings. This warning sign might seem like a minor inconvenience, but it is a caution to keep you from making costly mistakes.

In the same way, God placed "signposts" in your life to help guide you and keep you on the straight and narrow path. He warns you of dangers associated with wrong paths and offers you the opportunity to choose the right direction. His Word gives you clarity and direction. Satan might tempt you to take a shortcut [distractions] designed to lead you away from the path God has for you. Follow the path, God laid out for you, you will live a life of peace and contentment. Just like the "Do Not Enter-Wrong Way" sign, God's warning helps you avoid making wrong decisions and going down the wrong path. Trust in His plan for you.

Like God, your parents, and maybe a good friend has tried to warn you, but you ignored them. Only to find out they were telling you the truth. It might not have been what you wanted to hear, but it was true. Your emotional state of mind at the time may have lured you to a place of resentment and even hate for your parents or friend. You cut yourself, shaved your head, tattooed your body, gave up on life and perhaps attempted suicide. You feel alone, stressed, unworthy, rejected, and it's painful to be alive. That is not the voice of God you are hearing and it's not the voice of anyone who truly loves you. Do not enter these types of thoughts and suggestions Satan dangles in your mind because you don't acknowledge God.

In Romans 1:28 God warns us. I will take the liberty here to give you three different translations of this verse because it is important that you have a clear understanding.

> *"Just as they did not think it worthwhile to retain the knowledge of God, so God gave them over to a depraved mind, so that they do what ought not to be done." (NIV)*

> *"Since they thought it foolish to acknowledge God, he abandoned them to their foolish thinking and let them do things that should never be done." (NLT)*

> *"Since they did not see fit to acknowledge God, He gave them up to a depraved mind, to do what ought not to be done." (Berean Standard Bible)*

A deprave mind means the mind is morally corrupt and wicked. When you refuse to acknowledge God, you get entangled in Satan's entrapments. Satan has a way of putting you in the presence of people with a common thread of a depraved mind and they will keep you captured in thinking what you are doing is right. In order for you to be right, the Bible is wrong, and nothing more than a book of divisive literature written by a crew of men; or you will say the Bible is outdated and out of touch with reality. A depraved mind will even insinuate God created him/her in contradiction to His own Word! God is warning you if you do not see fit to acknowledge who He is, He will abandon you to your foolish thinking [choices] and He will let you do things that should never be done. God outlined the things you should never do in the Bible. God will never counsel you to do anything He directs you not to do in His Word. He will never lead you down a path of self-destruction.

Be careful of people who tell you what you want to hear to appease you. Be careful if the inner voice you hear tells you to do something you know is not right. When you do one thing you know is not right, before you know it you will have done a slew of things that aren't right. Before you know it, doing things that are not right and or proper become second nature to you. You do wrong and approve of it like there is no tomorrow. If you fall into traps that entangle you with Satan, to the point you disapprove of God's Word that's a problem. Make sure you read multiple times the chapters on backsliding, emergency exit, and lost and found for some helpful tips on what to do.

CHAPTER 8

The Road Ends Here: Maybe Not

Now is the time for you to understand Dead-End Roads and Life. Merriam Webster defines dead end, *"lacking opportunities especially for advancement, lacking an exit; the road will no longer proceed or take you further."* There may be a time in your life when following God felt like a dead-end. Surely, Moses thought he had reached a dead-end when he beat an Egyptian to death and hid his body in the sand. Moses, a murder! He killed the Egyptian when he saw him beating a Hebrew man without cause. He feared the consequences and fled to Midian. [Exodus 2:11-15] Shortly after Moses fled to Midian the dead-end road turned into a path of hope when he married Zipporah. [Exodus 2:21] Moses must have felt a sigh of relief when he learned the King of Egypt had died. What initially appeared to be a dead-end to Moses ended up being a new beginning.

The enslaved Israelites cried out for Help. God heard their cries. God was concerned, and He remembered his promise to Abraham, Isaac, and Jacob. Look at Exodus 3: 1-22:

> *"Moses was taking care of the sheep of his father-in-law Jethro, the priest of Midian. As he led the sheep to the far side of the desert, he came to Horeb, the mountain of God.[2] The Messenger of the Lord appeared to him there as flames of fire coming out of a bush. Moses looked, and although the bush was on fire, it was not burning up.[3] So he thought, "Why isn't this bush burning up? I must go over there and see this strange sight."[4] When the Lord saw that Moses had come over to see it, God called to him from the bush, "Moses, Moses! "Moses answered, "Here I am!"[5] God said, "Don't come any closer! Take off your sandals because this place where you are standing is holy ground.[6] I am the God of your ancestors, the God of Abraham, Isaac, and Jacob." Moses hid his face because he was afraid to look at God.[7] The Lord said, "I have seen the misery of my people in Egypt, and I have heard them crying out because of the slave drivers. I know how much they're suffering.[8] I have come to rescue them from the power of the Egyptians and to bring them from that land to a good land with plenty of room for everyone It is a land flowing with milk and honey where the Canaanites,*

Hittites, Amorites, Perizzites, Hivites, and Jebusites live.
⁹ I have heard the cry of the people of Israel. I have seen
how the Egyptians are oppressing them. ¹⁰ Now, go! I am
sending you to Pharaoh so that you can bring my people
Israel out of Egypt." ¹¹ But Moses said to God, "Who am I
that I should go to Pharaoh and bring the people of Israel
out of Egypt?" ¹² God answered, "I will be with you. And
this will be the proof that I sent you: When you bring the
people out of Egypt, all of you will worship God on this
mountain." ¹³ Then Moses replied to God, "Suppose I go
to the people of Israel and say to them, 'The God of your
ancestors has sent me to you,' and they ask me, 'What
is his name?' What should I tell them?" ¹⁴ God answered
Moses, "I Am Who I Am. This is what you must say to
the people of Israel: 'I Am has sent me to you.'" ¹⁵ Again
God said to Moses, "This is what you must say to the
people of Israel: The Lord God of your ancestors, the
God of Abraham, Isaac, and Jacob, has sent me to you.
This is my name forever. This is my title throughout
every generation.¹⁶ "Go, assemble the leaders of Israel.
Say to them, 'The Lord God of your ancestors, the God
of Abraham, Isaac, and Jacob, appeared to me. He said,
"I have paid close attention to you and have seen what
has been done to you in Egypt. ¹⁷ I promise I will take
you away from your misery in Egypt to the land of the
Canaanites, Hittites, Amorites, Perizzites, Hivites, and
Jebusites, a land flowing with milk and honey."'¹⁸ "The

leaders of Israel will listen to you. Then you and the leaders must go to the king of Egypt and say to him, 'The Lord God of the Hebrews has met with us. Please let us travel three days into the desert to offer sacrifices to the Lord our God.' ¹⁹ I know that the king of Egypt will not let you go, even if he is forced to. ²⁰ So I will use my power to strike Egypt. After all the miracles that I will do there, he will let you go. ²¹ I will make the Egyptians kind to the people of Israel so that, when you leave, you will not leave empty-handed.²² "Every Hebrew woman should ask her Egyptian neighbor and any woman living in her home for silver and gold jewelry and for clothes. Put them on your sons and daughters. This way you will strip Egypt of its wealth."

In these verses, God spoke to Moses. Moses's reaction: He hid his face. He was afraid to look at God. Just like Adam and Eve hid from God. Just like you hide from God. Hiding from God, appears to be a repeated behavior. But God moved passed Moses' insecurity and gave him a complicated assignment. The assignment was so out of Moses brain space; he asked God questions. He wanted to know what he should tell the people if they wanted to know God's name. He wanted to know what he should do if the people of Israel asked him who sent him. You can see from the verses above God answered Moses. Not only did God answer Moses, but He also assured Moses the King of Egypt would let them go After He struck Egypt and after all the miracles, He would do there. God gave an escape route for the Israelites that included them leaving Egypt where they were oppressed with wealth. An escape route that would have felt like a dead end once they reached the Red Sea.

How many times have you felt insecure about something God told you to do? Did you feel insecure or unworthy? I can think of a directive God gave me. Like Moses, I questioned God's instructions. I was called to Counsel Pastors. Me, a female? In a male driven church of Christ. Some Pastors believed women should not be in the pulpit? There are some churches where women cannot teach men. Some ultra-conservative churches feel women should be at home twiddling their thumbs, barefoot, pregnant, cooking, and cleaning. Surely, God was jesting with me. When God gave this directive, I had been counseling pastors and their congregations in my legal capacity for years. I counselled them collectively with Michigan Concerned Clergy. I did not get this vibe from most of the clergy there. This vibe predominantly came from the white conservative churches, but I must admit some black pastors read from the same script.

I had a laundry list of reasons God could not be pointing me down what seemed a dead-end road. In case you are wondering, reason number one: Why me? You have a million pastors, with a church on almost every corner they don't need me. Reason number two: I felt I was not seminary trained. God's response: "I trained and equipped you." My reaction: I enrolled in Ashland Theological Seminary, Master of Divinity Program. Like Moses, I was insecure. I was concerned about what the ministers would think and say. I still counsel pastors to this day, but not on the level God anointed and directed me to serve. It wasn't enough that I counselled multiple pastors and church congregations and handled their legal woes in court...so embarrassing when I think about their quarrels and disputes. I remained low key and hid hoping this directive would vanish. **IT DID NOT.**

In the verses discussed above, God chose Moses to lead the Israelites out of Egypt. Despite his insecurities and fear. The scripture details Moses doing what God instructed him to do. God delivered the Israelites from the oppressive hands of the Egyptians. But from the delivered Israelites point of view, it led them to a dead-end. When Pharoah's heart hardened, he rebelled and joined his men in hot pursuit of them. They stared down the face of the Red Sea with no boats or any other apparatus in sight to get them across. They felt forsaken and doomed. God true to His Word, parted the Red Sea and ushered them across. Their feet walked across the land at the bottom of the sea. While the Red Sea appeared to be a dead-end with no way for them to cross it, the signs we see, "Dead end no Turn around or Dead-end no thru traffic" may be just what the sign says for some people but not so for those God choose to provide an escape or exit plan for. Turning around was not an option for them. Sometimes it's not an option for you. Press forward and trust God. He has never forsaken you.

What happens when a road doesn't go any further? What do you do when the road ends and there's nowhere else to go? This is what it means to go down a dead-end road. Some people look at their job titles, roles, and responsibilities and conclude it's a glass ceiling. Do you feel you have gone as far as you can with your current job? Do you struggle with drugs and alcohol addiction, hitting your "rock bottom" may be your end of the road. Maybe this traffic sign is God's way of testing your faith. In dead-end situations, your first thought might consider going down a dead-end road as a negative experience. After all, it can seem like a metaphor for "hitting a wall" or reaching a point in life where progress is no longer possible. But a dead-end road can be an opportunity to take a step back and think about what direction you should take next. It can be a reminder to look for fresh paths and new opportunities to keep growing and learning.

The Bible speaks to this idea, emphasizing the importance of staying focused on the ultimate destination: eternal life. In Proverbs 23:18 says, *"For surely there is an end; and thine expectation shall not be cut off."* This verse says, no matter what path you are on your hope will not be cut off. But even on a dead-end road, you can keep your eyes fixed on your ultimate destination and use the situation to further progress in your journey of faith. You may see a dead-end road as a chance to pause and assess your current course, as well as an opportunity to seek alternative paths. While a dead-end road or a dead-end life may appear to be the end of the line, the Bible encourages you to keep moving forward on your spiritual journey.

Ecclesiastes 7:8-9 says, *"Better is the end of a thing than the beginning thereof: and the patient in spirit is better than the proud in spirit. Be not hasty in thy spirit to be angry: for anger rest in the bosom of fools."* Even when you are stuck in a difficult situation, you can find your way out and continue to move forward, no matter where your journey takes you, the Bible encourages you to have faith and to keep your eyes fixed on the ultimate destination–eternal life. God is always there to guide you, even when you feel you are at a dead end with no way out. He leads you on a journey to an even better path, but it requires your faith and trust in Him. Jesus said, "I am the way, the truth, and the life. No one comes to the Father except through me" [John 14:6].

Rather than giving up or feeling hopeless when faced with a dead end, turn to God, and ask Him to show you the way out. Seek Him in prayer with His Word. He will provide a solution. You are not crazy! And don't let anyone tell you, you are. You may suffer emotionally, or have a medically diagnosed mental health disorder. This does not make you less desirable, ruined, or unworthy. If God can use a murderer, He can use you!

God promised He will never forsake you. He will give you the courage and strength to move forward on the path He has chosen for you. God is always looking out for you. Leaving a dead-end road may not be the most direct or comfortable route, but it will lead to a brighter future. Follow God and don't be afraid to take a new road. He has grand plans in store for you. Trust Him and you'll soon find yourself in a beautiful and fulfilling place, far from the dead-end road you once faced.

For some, a dead-end road can be a place of both fear and despair-especially when there is no turnaround looming ahead you can see with your physical eyesight. It can be a place of missed opportunities where you feel your life is stagnant and stuck. Don't be afraid, for there may be a fresh path in store that can bring you hope and joy. When you feel trapped on a dead-end road and you can't seem to find your way out, it is critical that you turn to the greatest source of hope and renewal: God! He has splendid plans for you. God gave you the chance to be reborn and pray your way out of whatever situation you are in.

God's plan for you may provide a completely different roadway that will fulfill you and bring you happiness. It will be far from the dead-end road you once thought you were on. God will provide joy and blessings beyond what you ever hoped or expected. God's aim for your life is to bring you comfort whatever your current situation may be. It takes faith and courage to trust in God's plan for your life, but it is worth it. You can never know what amazing blessings He has in store for you until you take the leap of faith and expect Him to bring you out of your dead-end traffic jam into a place of eternal rest.

Re-evaluate some decisions and choices you made that play apart in making you feel you hit a dead end. Maybe you volunteer for an organization that has snuffed out all of your free relaxation time and competes with your balanced finances by requiring you to pay to volunteer. Maybe it steers you to prey on people you know to convince them to give of their resources to the volunteer effort that you are partaking in.

You may find yourself in organizations and churches that can become just one more thing to break you and send you in a downward spiral. Some people seek self-worth or validation in the activities they engage in only to find they have neglected their marriage, family, members, and friends. This may be your dead-end because your ego won't let you get rid of stuff because you have invested your time and resources into supporting the goals and objectives of the organization that has nothing to do with God's call on your life. The book of Haggai will give you information regarding the outcome of putting your money into bags with holes.

Take a deep sigh of relief. You learned earlier in this book you can Stop here for Jesus and spend time in his presence. He will give you the right answers to your dilemma. Trust God. He will direct your path. When you come across a No Thru Traffic Dead End sign, you know you can't go any further in that direction. The sign is a warning to find a different route. However, for your eternal destination, you may take a road with a dead end. God is very direct when he warns you there is no thru traffic here, and you are at a dead end.

For those who choose not to repent, or put their trust in Jesus Christ, their destination is eternal conscious torment. Theologians have long known the metaphor of a dead end to describe the fate of someone who goes through life without a relationship with God. There is no turning back once they cross the line from the living to the eternal dead. As the Bible states, "He that covers his sin shall not prosper." As believers, it is our job to help others learn to turn away from this dead end.

You must do your part to warn others of the consequences of choosing sin over righteousness. Remind them of the love God has for them and the opportunity He gives them to turn away from their sins and seek restoration. God has given you a warning sign that says No Thru Traffic Dead End. Take the time to heed the message and help those headed on an eternal dead-end road. Through your efforts and prayers, you can help bring them out of darkness and into the light of eternal life in Jesus Christ. The reality of the no thru traffic dead end sign can be both dangerous and heartbreaking. For some, it may lead to a physical and emotional roadblock difficult to overcome. For others, it may signify a spiritual dead end, where the hope of a better life gets replaced with despair and helplessness. In these situations, we must all be active participants in providing our family, neighbors and friends with the hope and care they need to escape their dead ends.

As members of a caring community, we must be aware and take action to heed the message of hope and help those headed down a toilet stool path to nowhere. Through our collective prayers, we can provide help and support so each person can find their way back to a life of joy and purpose. At the heart of our efforts must be the love and care of Jesus Christ, who offers a hope and a future to anyone who reaches out to Him. He provides the ultimate escape from darkness and desperation, directing our feet onto a path of eternal life and joy.

We must be ready to share His love and truth with those who are struggling in their dead-end situations. By focusing on care and compassion, we can help bring those stuck in an eternal dead end out of the darkness and into the light of Jesus Christ. Our commitment to caring for one another, as brothers and sisters in Christ, is essential for breaking the chains of despair and offering everlasting hope to our neighbors in need. I recently discussed scripture in 1 Timothy 2:1-8 during our bible study class, we discussed God's expectation that we pray for all men. You should not pick who you decide to pray for because you don't like certain people. God wants us to pray for all men. He desires that all men get saved. I know it's hard to imagine you will be in heaven with some mean and nasty people who you feel don't deserve to be there.

We learned when we pray for our enemies and people we don't like, it gives us peace and calm. You can sleep a worry-free night. If you just do what God directs you to do, you can help lead people from a dark sinful life on to what we hope would be a dead-end road toward Jesus… no turning back and away from God. Let the path of righteousness be your dead-end road to heaven.

CHAPTER 9

For some people, Caution signs are like deer with headlights. The Bible has at least one hundred scriptures about being cautious. It is important that you remain vigilant and take caution signs you see on the road and other areas serious. Whether it's a warning of a hazardous area or a reminder to look both ways when crossing the street, caution signs are essential for keeping you and society safe. Being cautious can save you from life-or-death situations. You should know what you do, why you do it, when you do it, how you do it, so be conscious of potential risks. This includes paying attention to traffic signals and warning signs God give you to avoid traffic jams that pop up in your life. God cautioned you to think about your plan of action, control your emotions, and avoid harmful situations.

I John 4:1 cautions you not to believe every spirit. It says: *"Beloved, do not believe every spirit, but test the spirits to see whether they are from God, for many false prophets have gone out into the world."* In this verse, God warns you that many false prophets are in the world today. This means there are people who falsely claim the gift of prophecy or divine inspiration or to speak for God, or who makes such claims for evil ends. The New Testament shows the antichrist is a false prophet that denies and or don't believe in the messiahship of Jesus. There are deceitful people in this world today who will use the name of Jesus to get what they want from you. Yes, they will scam you, destroy you, and even kill you for their own pleasure or gain. If you are not studying the bible, reading the word, or praying to God, how will you know when to be cautious, where to be cautious, or how to be cautious? You must be cautious. False prophets in the world stand up in church and other sacred places and speak to you. They will falsely tell you what God has told them regarding your life. How will you know a true prophet from a false one?

Jeremiah 6:13, 27:14 says, false prophets prophesied lies. They deceived people with their dreams, Jeremiah 29:8. The false prophets threatened the lives of the true prophets, Jeremiah 26:7. There are some false prophets that use magic: Ezekiel 13:17-23. There were others that used divination, soothsaying, witchcraft, necromancy, and sorcery that were forbidden. Today Satan has desensitized you. Sorcery, wizards, witches, and witchcraft, portrayed in epic proportions on the big screens grab your attention and excites you. They have lured you away from caution. So, when God tells you to be cautious because the adversary will come like a thief in the night, you may chuckle and say "BOO" because you don't believe that witches, and sorcerers, really exist. Many people have heard about these things, but they don't believe them.

False prophets: will tell you what you want to hear they brainwash you, Ezekiel 13:10-12; Ezekiel 13:14-15, 22:28. God warns you to be cautious beyond the Old and New Testament accounts. God warned believers to test persons who make prophetic claims today. An easy way to call out a false prophet is if he/she denies Jesus has come in the flesh, that person is not a true prophet from God 1 John 4:1-3. Matthew 24:1; 24:24; Revelation 16: 13-14; 20:20 warns you to be cautious in the end-times. These false prophets will deceive you to get you to follow Satan: "the beast" they will even perform miracles and signs. The Good news is Christ return will destroy the entire institution of false prophecy. Revelation 19:20 confirms this: *"And the beast was captured, along with the false prophet who in its presence had done the signs by which he deceived those who had received the mark of the beast and those who worshipped its image. These two were thrown alive into the lake of fire that burns with sulfur."*

As you see in 2 Peter 1:16-21, It is said that no prophecy was ever produced by the will of man, but the Holy Spirit enabled man to speak from God.

Christ's Glory and the Prophetic Word

16 For we did not follow cleverly devised myths when we made known to you the power and coming of our Lord Jesus Christ, but we were eyewitnesses of his majesty. 17 For when he received honor and glory from God the Father, and the voice was borne to him by the Majestic Glory, "This is my beloved Son, with whom I am well pleased," 18 we ourselves heard this very voice borne from heaven, for we were with him on the holy mountain. 19 And we have the prophetic word more fully confirmed, to which you will do well to pay attention as to a lamp shining in a dark place, until the day dawns and the morning star rises in your hearts, **20** *knowing this first of all, that no prophecy of Scripture comes from someone's own interpretation.* **21** *For no prophecy was ever produced by the will of man, but men spoke from God as they were carried along by the Holy Spirit."*

You should not be cautious by accident. You must always be on alert: *"One who is wise is cautious and turns away from evil, but a fool is reckless and careless.* Proverbs 14:16. Take caution and ensure that you are saved. *"I appeal to you therefore, brothers, by the mercies of God, to present your bodies as a living sacrifice, holy and acceptable to God, which is your spiritual worship,"* Romans 12:1.

Caution to those who believe in God, and profess to be His, and has world's good, sees his brother in need, yet closes his heart against him, how does God's love abide in him? [1 John 3:17] This caution is a barometer from God. It keeps you real about who you claim to be versus who you truly are. God is saying when you see someone in need you should not ignore the need or turn away from your brother. Be like the good Samaritan who did not cross on the other side of the street when he saw a man lying there helpless. You may see a person with a sign saying: "I will work for food" or another sign saying: "help." Do you talk about the person, shrug your shoulders, and tell them to get a job? Does God's love abide in you?

God cautions a lazy person who does nothing but look for handouts. Proverbs 10:4 says: "a slack hand causes poverty, but the hand of the diligent makes rich." Proverbs 13:4 says: *"The soul of the sluggard craves and gets nothing, while the soul of the diligent is richly supplied."* You have heard the saying that some people have champagne taste and Kool-Aid money. It's easy to have an attitude when you are a hardworking person who works hard for every penny you earn to have someone beg you for money at the gas station or grocery store when they appear able bodied. Just remember 1 Timothy 5:8: "But if anyone does not provide for his relatives, and especially for members of his household, he has denied the faith and is worse than an unbeliever." Consider this, if the relatives of the man or woman who approached you begging for money for food would have helped them, maybe they would not approach strangers. This may be an unwinnable argument. *"Give to the one who begs from you and do not refuse the one who would borrow from you."* [Matthew 5:42]

We are busy people and it's easy for us to get busy doing multiple things. Volunteering, donating food, money, clothing, and whatever else you do. But for who and what reason? If you are doing what you are doing to give God the Glory, Then give God the Glory. If it's making an organization, club, or group look good then give them the credit, but be clear about that. Don't say that through the organization, club, or activity you are doing it for God.

Parents should teach their children the importance of obeying caution signs and lead by example. Take caution while watching and praying over your loved one's lives. Be proactive protect the one's you love and keep your environment safe and positive. Overall, you should take seriously caution in all aspects of life. If you pay attention to potential risks and distractions, God will protect you and those you love. Put your own risk management plan in action. Always take a few moments to think before you act. By following these tips, you will remain open eyed and ready for any potential risks that comes your way.

You must heed caution signs at home, work, and in public. Caution signs are visual warnings designed to alert you. From warning signs for wet floors to signs showing dangerous heights, these signs are an integral part of creating a safe environment. You should be cautious with information you share on the internet and social media platforms. Be vigilant about who you share personal information with. Back in the day, people kept their business and family matters private. Nowadays, people are living Open book lives. You don't even have to turn the pages to know what is going on in their life. You already know what is on the next page.

Do people really need to see and know all of your business? God has given you caution signs, and it's important to take these signs seriously. He gives you these warnings for your safety and well-being. He highlights areas that may be hazardous to your health if not handled with care. Like getting your prostate checked, colonoscopy, cancer screenings, heart check. Dental checkups and other medical checkups you have avoided despite God's warning. Failing to respect the caution signs God sends can put your life, other people, and property at risk.

We all have a responsibility to pay attention to caution signs. Being aware of them can save lives. It may be your life that is saved. This includes slowing down when a warning sign is present and, waiting for traffic to pass before crossing the street, or taking extra steps to prevent the spread of illnesses. It may mean waiting for a situation or circumstance to blow over before you act irrationally from your emotions.

It may be calming down and getting yourself and anger under control before you do or say something you can't take back or change.

God provides many caution signs in the bible to help you pay attention to your surroundings. God commands us to love one another like we love ourselves. He knows differences in opinions can cause people to roar with anger and hate. But He cautions you to love your brothers and sisters. God is not behind the hate people espoused toward one another. But His wrath will fall upon man because of his sinful actions and deeds. In James 1: 19 He said: "Let every person be quick to hear, slow to speak, slow to anger; for the anger of man does not produce the righteousness of God." *"The reward for humility and fear of the Lord is riches and honor and life."* [Proverbs 22:4] following these tips, will keep you on guard and conscious of potential risks while keeping you and your family, friends, and environment safe.

Failure to observe caution signs may lead to serious consequences or injuries so, think before you act. You can prevent many incidents from occurring. Look out for installed caution signs. These are blue or yellow and provide a clear warning of potential hazards. Examples of caution signs include damp floor, slippery surface, or hazardous activity. Sometimes, caution signs are accompanied by other warning methods such as yellow tape, signs, or safety cones. Be sure to observe these warnings they are there to keep you safe.

Man ignored God's first warning in the Garden of Eden. Most know the story well. But that disobedient act came at a significant cost. Jesus warned against sin and evil. In Luke 12:15 KJV "And he said unto them, take heed, and beware of covetousness: For *man's life consisteth not in the abundance of the things which he possesseth." In the ESV…"* And *he said to them, Take care, and be on your guard again…"* God warns about the Antichrist: 2 Thessalonians 2:3-5:

> ³*"Let no man deceive you by any means: for that day shall not come, except there comes a falling away first, and that man of sin be revealed, the son of perdition. ⁴ Who opposeth and exalteth himself above all that is called God, or that is worshipped; so that he as God sitteth in the temple of God, shewing himself that he is God.⁵ Remember ye not, that, when I was yet with you, I told you these things?"*

God warns about sins that separate us from Him. Isaiah 59:2

> *"Your iniquities have become a separation between you and your God, and your sins have hidden his face from you so that He does not hear."*

God warns about the last days Genesis 49: 1; Matthew 24; Mark 13, and Luke 21 and Revelation. He warns about the Counterfeit Christ 2 Peter 1:19:

> *We also have the prophetic message as something completely reliable, and you will do well to pay attention to it, as to a light shining in a dark place, until the day dawns and the morning star rises in your hearts".*

2 Peter 2:18:

> *"For they mouth empty, boastful words and, by appealing to the lustful desires of the flesh, they entice*

people who are just escaping from those who live in error."

More messages of caution you should read: God warns about Backsliding [Colossians 2:8]. He warns about Jealousy, Money, and Greed in [1Corinthians 13:5; Hebrews 13:5] God also warns about laziness/slothfulness [Proverbs 10:4; Ecclesiastes 9:10; Proverbs 12:24, and Proverbs 13:4].

CHAPTER 10

Are you feeling overwhelmed by life lately? Are your days often rushed, filled with too much to do and too little time to do it? If so, it may be time to SLOW DOWN. Foremost, SLOW DOWN and make time for yourself and your mental, emotional, and spiritual wellbeing. Take a few moments each day to reflect, meditate and just be in the present moment. Allow yourself the time to connect with God and fill your life with peace and joy. Fasting can be a great way to SLOW DOWN and refocus on the important things in life. By abstaining from sex, certain food, or beverages, you can draw closer to God and recalibrate your priorities.

The Bible calls us to SLOW DOWN and remember our need Psalm 46:10, *reads "Be still, and know that I am God; I will be exalted among the nations, I will be exalted in the earth."* This lets you know God is sovereign and you can trust Him with all of your concerns. Examining how you speak can help you SLOW DOWN. When you talk quickly, you miss out on important conversations and misunderstandings can arise. Taking the time to articulate your thoughts with care and thinking about the words you choose can help you appreciate one another's perspectives.

SLOW DOWN and make time for self-care, fasting, reflecting on God's sovereignty, and speaking clearly are excellent ways to intentionally slow down and stay acquainted with your faith and priorities. it's difficult to put into practice the often-heard advice to "slow down." With the hustle and bustle of everyday life, you can quickly become overwhelmed. Fortunately, slowing down and staying acquainted with your faith and your priorities is an attainable goal if you make the effort.

One way to slow down is to focus on getting enough sleep, taking walks, journaling, meditating, or engaging in other activities that bring you comfort. This will allow you time to decompress and regroup so you're ready to tackle challenges and tasks with a refreshed outlook. Fasting is another great way to slow down and connect with God and your spiritual self. It's the practice of abstaining from food and other pleasures for a period. In the Bible, we often connect fasting to prayer and meditation. By abstaining from everyday things, we're used to doing, we can get in touch with our innermost thoughts and feelings, get closer to God, and learn to prioritize what's truly important.

Reflecting on God's sovereignty is also a great way to slow down and appreciate the gifts He's given you. When you acknowledge God's control over your life, it can put into perspective just how limited your power without God truly is. We can take comfort in the fact God's plans for us are good. What we say and how we say it along with how we speak to people is important. Speaking mindfully is critical for slowing down. Take time to really think before you speak. Consider the motives behind your words and the impact they may have. How can you make sure your words are kind and full of love?

This minimalist approach to communication is often much more effective than speaking without thinking. Your faith and priorities can be maintained if you put in the effort to practice reflecting on God's sovereignty and speaking mindfully. These steps, taken collectively, will help you become disciplined in your faith and your priorities so you can live a life pleasing to God. It does not take much to be overwhelmed in our fast-paced world to find yourself pulled in many directions and neglect your mental and spiritual wellbeing.

Instead of constantly rushing through life, dedicate moments to sit in stillness and calm. Allow yourself to relax and think about how you spend your time. Rely on God's love and view life as a blessing. When you bring your awareness to the present moment, you will be better able to appreciate all you have. Take a break throughout your day to pray and check on yourself. Indulge in activities that bring you joy like reading, journaling, or creating. Allow yourself to be creative and experiment with new hobbies or skills. Taking the time to do something enjoyable will remind you, your life is a gift to be celebrated.

When you communicate with other people, speak words of peace, kindness, and love. Pay close attention to how you speak and react. Instead of being quick to judge, respond with grace and understanding. Slowing down doesn't mean you have to stop being productive. You can still reach your goals at a comfortable, sustainable pace. Eliminate the unnecessary stress and know your growth and success will come in due time. So, slow down and take time to explore your life. Allow yourself to relax and take pleasure in taking care of yourself. Be mindful of your words and deeds. In doing so, you will make the most out of your life. No toilet stool life—no drama filled crap in and crap out!

NEVER BE TO BUSY TO MAKE TIME FOR GOD

We should not underestimate the importance of carving out time for God every day. No matter how busy life may get, it is essential to make time for God. Because it will provide you with the spiritual nourishment, you need to move forward in life and to approach each day with a positive attitude and outlook. You may be familiar with the story of the two sisters Mary and Martha. Martha was so busy trying to serve that she took offense when her sister Mary recognizing who Jesus is, used her time with Him wisely and sat at his feet. Luke 10:38-42 gives this account:

> *"Now as they went on their way, Jesus entered a village. And a woman named Martha welcomed him into her house. And she had a sister called Mary, who sat at the Lord's feet and listened to his teaching. But Martha was distracted with much serving. And she went up to him and said, "Lord, do you not care that my sister has left me to serve alone? Tell her then to help me." But the Lord answered her, "Martha, Martha, you are anxious and troubled about many things, but one thing is necessary. Mary has chosen the good portion, which will not be taken away from her."*

Isaiah 55:6 says: "Seek the Lord while he may be found; call upon him while he is *near*."

Believers who serve in church particularly during the praise and worship services should take this scripture to heart. I suspect people wouldn't know what to do if everyone were suddenly required to stop moving about the church in such urgency and busyness when the Pastor delivers the message from God. You can get caught up ushering, singing, dancing, monitoring the computer screens, counting money, and doing other tasks that distract you from hearing the Word of God. Unfortunately, this busyness serves as a distraction to the congregants as they watch you constantly move about the sanctuary. If you can't get peace and rest at church, where else can you get it? God says:

> *"Come to me, all who labor and are heavy laden, and I will give you rest. Take my yoke upon you, and learn from me, for I am gentle and lowly in heart, and you will find rest for your souls. For my yoke is easy, and my burden is light."* [Matthew 11:28-30]

Some people come to church like David for a Word from God. People come asking God in prayer for answers, and they sit on the pew Sunday morning expecting to hear an answer from God. In Psalm 143.8 David prayed: *"Let me hear in the morning of your steadfast love, for in you I trust. Make me know the way I should go, for to you I lift up my soul."* In verses 7-12, David prays that God would be pleased with him, and he wanted God to let him know this. David wanted to be enlightened with the knowledge of God's Will. This is first the work of the Holy Spirit. As David didn't simply pray to be enlightened but he wanted

God to not only show him the right way but to teach him how to do it. You have the Lord, your God and the Holy Spirit to guide you.

Prayer is the most important way to interact with God. You have the opportunity to open up to Him and discuss your feelings. Through prayer, you find comfort, guidance, and reassurance from God's limitless understanding and love. If you lack wisdom, ask God, He gives generously to all without reproach, ask and it will be given to you. [James 1:5]

Prayer gives you peace and a greater awareness of what is truly important in your life. Through prayer you find your true purpose. Daily time with God keeps you aware of His presence in your life. With this awareness, you recognize the many blessings and opportunities available to you and you are encouraged to appreciate the moments of contentment. Prayer strengthens your faith and helps you to put your trust in God in the darkest of times. while praying, you stay rooted in God's Word. Meditating on the Word of God, gives your mental, emotional, and spiritual health balance.

When you pray God is in control of all of your struggles and challenges, no matter how big or small. No matter how busy your life may get, you must make God first and talk to Him each day. You will see your blessings. Stay engaged in communication with God in prayer, and remain spiritually nourished You will move forward. Approach each day with readiness, expectancy, and gratitude.

There are endless demands and distractions that pull you away from your spiritual worship and makes it difficult for you to find time for God. I get it! Understand how you would feel if God did not have time for you 2-4-7. God provides you with the source of love and hope and He knows the world and the struggles you go through when you try to go it alone and do things without Him. When you devote time to thank God, worship, and praise Him, you become centered and present in your day-to-day spiritual life. Talk to God, and listen to His guidance. When he says Slow Down, He is also saying:

> *"Therefore, I tell you, do not be anxious about your life, what you will eat or what you will drink, nor about your body, what you will put on. Is not life more than food, and the body more than clothing? Look at the birds of the air: they neither sow nor reap nor gather into barns, and yet your heavenly Father feeds them. Are you not of more value than they? And which of you by being anxious can add a single hour to his span of life? And why are you anxious about clothing? Consider the lilies of the field, how they grow: they neither toil nor spin, yet I tell you, even Solomon in all his glory was not arrayed like one of these. But if God so clothes the grass of the field, which today is alive and tomorrow is thrown into the oven, will he not much more clothe you, O you of little faith? Therefore, do not be anxious, saying, 'What shall we eat? Or what shall we drink? Or what shall we wear? For the Gentiles seek after all these things, and your heavenly Father knows that you need them. But seek first the kingdom of God and his righteousness, and all of these things will be added to you. Therefore, do not be anxious about tomorrow, for tomorrow will be anxious itself, Sufficient for the day is its own trouble. [Matthew 6:25-34]*

As you can see, God cautions you to slow down, and He will help you stay focused on the right path and bring you peace and solace in difficult times. Finding time for God does not have to be an arduous task. Your life can be incredibly fulfilling and purposeful when you take the time to strengthen your faith. One way to make time for God each day is to schedule and commit to time for prayer. even if it's a few minutes at a time. This could be anything from a heartfelt conversation with God to a quick statement expressing gratitude. You open yourself up to spiritual growth and a closer relationship with Him. You set yourself up to become more mindful and in tune with your faith, leading you to a more fulfilling and purposeful life. God, a greater power than you, takes care of you. That is a gift.

There are many activities you engage in that take up enormous amounts of time. Sorority and fraternity life can be a huge distraction. They command your time, talent, and financial resources regularly. It becomes a problem when it becomes your God when you hold it nearer and dearer to your heart than God. When you sacrifice time spent with God for activities and programs that pull you away, it's time to make some God prioritizing decisions. I have a saying, "where your time is spent, is where your money went." Attending athletic games can be a time stealer too. Whatever gets your attention and requires you to spend less time with God, is a problem. Worship God. Whether it's attending a physical or virtual church service, taking part in a zoom Bible study, or simply listening to spiritual music, and worship, this keeps your faith and trust in God.

If you are not a church goer on any level, It could be helpful for you to get involved in a local church or faith-based community. Taking part in evangelizing activities with others can be a great way to deepen your relationship with God and to create a strong support system. When you make time for God, you can access deeper reserves of energy, strength, and resilience. A strengthened relationship between your body, mind, and soul gives you the tools, you need to better care for yourself. No matter how busy your life may be, it is always important to make time for God. By doing so, you not only take care of your spiritual well-being but also enhance your overall physical and mental health.

DO YOU STEAL JESUS FROM YOUR CHILDREN?

I grew up believing in Santa Claus and all of his reindeer. I have fond memories of Carmel, Jelly, Chocolate, Coconut, and Banana cakes; Sweet potato pies, Peach cobbler, Blackberry cobbler, Bread pudding, Rice pudding, Mac and cheese, Chitterlings, Hog maws, Glazed ham, Prime rib, Turkey with dressing, Collard greens, Cornbread, Crackling bread, Fried corn, and sometimes fried chicken aromas filled every room of our house while Santa's elves made loud banging noises putting together the Christmas toys. The adults, late at night, and in the wee hours of the morning were doing so much work in anticipation Santa was coming with lots of toys and goodies on his sleigh.

My siblings and I would sit at the top of the stairs peeking through the banister rails hoping to get a glimpse of a present or two. We would holler down the stairs from time to time asking, "can we come down now?" only to hear "No" time and time again. We were told Santa would not come until we went to sleep. When we finally woke up, my dad would tell us to hurry over to the window to see Santa and his reindeer flying off our rooftop. I closed one eye, opened them both and could never see Santa or his reindeer flying off our roof. Eventually I lied because my dad said if we didn't see Santa on the rooftop that meant we did not believe in Santa and would not get gifts. He said only those who believed could see Santa. Sounds familiar, doesn't it? Only those who believe in Christ can see Him. When I had my children, I replaced Santa with Jesus. I told them "You need to pray and ask Jesus to bless your parents financially so they can bless you with Christmas gifts." I wanted them to know Christmas gifts weren't from a make-believe stranger and we had to work to provide them. However, I wasn't consistent with the Tooth Fairy, or Easter bunny I allowed them to believe the fictitious tooth fairy exchanged money for their teeth. We didn't really celebrate or discuss the Easter bunny, but we colored eggs and hid them. It's weird I never thought about rabbits not laying eggs. I didn't really allow my children to take part in Halloween as far as it related to dressing up like hideous maiming evil characters depicting Satan. Trick or treating was pretty much at home or church. But you can see how we contradict who the true giver is and reflect on the wrong messages during holidays.

Flipping the script, I turned into one of those parents who wanted to bless my children. I wanted to provide them with things I never had during my childhood. I wanted them to be happy. Happiness sometimes meant providing things they wanted and allowing them to do some things they wanted to do. I was so busy giving it led my children to look to me for things and not God. They asked me and their father for stuff and we didn't direct them to ask Jesus [outside of Christmas gifts]. Now our children who know God, depend on us to make things happen for them, not God. Not to mention we have raised some children who feel entitled. Sometimes, I honestly believe we unintentionally taught our children to depend on us and not God. Yes, we took them to church and led by example by being actively involved in praise and worship during service. We attended bible study and studied at home too. I attended Ashland Theological Seminary to get a Master of Divinity degree. Not that we weren't praying and worshipping God as parents... we didn't allow our children to have a need or want that required them to seek Jesus and ask him.

We, like most parents, didn't teach them to ask God to identify his purpose for them to them. Most times we steered our children toward careers, dreams, and aspirations they identified, or we thought was best for them. We didn't steer our children toward titles and careers in God's Kingdom. We didn't suggest that they preach or teach. We didn't suggest that they consider becoming a pastor, evangelist, minister of music, teacher, church administrator, deacon, elder, or any position in the church not listed here. Some parents would rather for their sons and daughters to be professional ball players or hockey players. Some even trained their children to be entertainers hoping they would find fame and fortune at the risk of selling their souls to the devil. Sometimes our children who chased worldly dreams suffered turmoil, stress, and pain behind the scenes. They were no longer living a life that pleased God. Some became icons worshipped by fans and they were pushed to the limit for financial gain.

The Jacksons' worked diligently hard and persevered for a lifestyle where their children would be on top of the world despite sacrifices. We ponder what happened in the end to our beloved Michael, Prince, Whitney, and many other incredible people who left a mark on society because of their stardom. So many of our beloved celebrities have succumbed to alcohol and drugs that shortened their life. Whoever imagined such incredible people with God-given talents and spiritual gifts were like pearls cast before swine…entertaining people for money and being controlled by the money theyearned from ticket. A star's life in my humble opinion is no longer their own. They must sometimes invent drama and lies to stay relevant. Some of them arguably have become caught up in the limelight and God is nowhere on their radar.

They enticed us to be a part of their world. Whatever world was for them became that world for many of our children. When we do not provide opportunities for our children to keep them grounded in the Lord, we allow them to flirt with Satan's false dreams and promises where they will ultimately lose their life. They used their talents to leave God's children astray over to the dark side out of the light. I recently listened to the lyrics of a very talented and gifted songwriter and singer, who sings with soul beyond my belief, but the lyrics of his song surprised me. While riding in my daughter's car this Christmas season, the songs she grooved to and liked had very offensive lyrics, MF and the B word was almost every other word. My heart grieved because this is not good. Satan has our children thinking and or believing they can have one foot in holiness and righteousness while the other one promotes sin.How did we as parents allow this to happen? Our children don't trust us like they trust their friends. They take counsel from their peers who know no more than they do. Training our children in the way they should go…meant in "the Way" the only "Way." The path should be a one-way path to God. No hot and cold, maybe today or tomorrow stuff. To the new parents, and parents to be, think about how you as a parent will play an intricate role in training your children to love God with all of their hearts; to see themselves holding the hand of God at all times seeking to please Him and only Him. Nurture them in the Word of God and help them find their voice and place in His kingdom. Teach them to seek His face and His glory and assure them when they seek the kingdom of God all things will be added unto them. Teach your children how to pray. How to ask God for the desires of their heart. Show them answered prayer. Show them when God answers and provides for you. Our children need to know we have limitations, but God does not. They need to know we are nothing without God.

Think about the noble children God gifted you with. Our children come with a blank slate. It gets either refreshed or plagued with all the stuff we dump on them that does not align with who they are and who God called them to be. You should pray and fast with them so they can grow in God's Word and get to know Him for their self. I was tickled pink when my grandson told me he was going to tell Jesus on me because he did not like me telling him No about something. I was glad to know he knows a higher authority than me, God! He knows God is over my head and He knows God can do anything, even make me change my "No" to a "Yes."

Slow down and never be too busy for your kids. If you don't groom them while they are young, you may never get the chance to do so when they are adults. Make sure you don't contribute to making a toilet stool life for them.

CHAPTER 11

One day, you will make hard decisions and choices "yield not to temptation." 1 John 2:15-17 says:

> *Do not love the world or the things in the world. If anyone loves the world, the love of the Father is not in him. For all that is in the world—the desires of the flesh and the desires of the eyes and pride of life—is not from the Father but is from the world. And the world is passing away along with its desires, but whoever does the will of God abides forever.*

This particular scripture is a hard pill to swallow. Much of your life is entwined with earthly desires and pleasures. This scripture firmly admonishes those who love the world and the things in it. The world does not care about God and His sovereignty. That is why it is passing away along with its desires. Christians are called to always be mindful of our faith and rely on the Holy Spirit's guidance. This means when confronted with temptation, you should not yield. This is especially important when engaging in ministry. People can be tricky, and it's often hard to gauge their intentions or even how to react to them. Lean on God's wisdom and discernment and trust He will lead you in the right direction. It is necessary for your own good and the good of others to remember that in moments of temptation, your power to stop lies in yielding to God's Will.

If you walk by the Spirit, you will not gratify the desires of your flesh. You know from reading Galatians 5:16-17, *"that the desires of the flesh are against the Spirit, and the desires of the Spirit are against the flesh, for these are opposed to each other, to keep you from doing the things you want to do."*

God will guide you through uncharted waters and protect you from harm's way. When you are tempted to do something, you know is wrong, it's better to divert your attention elsewhere and rely on God's unchanging character and truth. When engaging in ministry service, remember God is the one in control. He will lead you and provide you with the means to use your spiritual gifts and abilities. Your heavenly Father is always watching over you and ready to help you through any situation. Trust God's guidance and seek His will for how to handle the challenging decisions life throws your way. Remember, in such times like these, to slow down, take a deep breath, yield, and trust God.

Put your trust in God's leadership to ensure the decisions you make are aligned with His Will. Before acting, it is important to yield and pause and consider the implications of your choices. It is wise to seek wise counsel from trusted mentors and clergy, and to pray for clarity and insight. The Bible is full of examples of individuals who trusted in God and proceeded with caution. Proverbs 3:5-6, *"trust in the Lord with all your heart and lean not on your own understanding; in all your ways acknowledge him, and he will make your paths straight."* Easier said than done may be your immediate reaction. It's hard to trust when you have been burned repeatedly. Friends played you for a fool. Spouse cheated on you. You prayed and nothing happened. You needed money to pay your rent, and everyone let you down. No one helped you when your car was down. You don't understand how people claim to love the Lord, but treat you like crap. Even though the bible says, *"These people honor me with their lips, but their heart is far from me."* [Matthew 15:8] You feel like toilet stools around the world are overflowing and only God can flush out the stinky mess. You can be confident He will provide the wisdom and understanding you need to make sound decisions.

Spend time in prayer and meditation. Think about who you are in Christ, *"I have been crucified with Christ. It is no longer I who live, but Christ who lives in me. And the life I now live in the flesh I live by faith in the Son of God, who loved me and gave himself for me."* [Galatians 2:20]

Christ died on the cross for you. He loved you so much that he gave his life. He paid the price for you therefore "No weapons formed against you shall prosper." [Isaiah 54:17] When other people forsake you, slap a "Black Sheep" label on you; speak dirt against you; take from you, and mistreat you, they won't get away with it. God sees and knows everything. You don't have to retaliate.

Ask God for direction and guidance and listen for His answer. He ensures you are taking the right steps in every phase of your life including your ministry. God said: *"I know the plans I have for you, declares the*

Lord, plans for welfare and not for evil, to give you a future and a hope." [Jeremiah 29:11] Don't you think you need to ask God about his plans for you? You can't run around this earth ignoring the greatness that you possess. Not knowing the significance of your life that can ignite the flame in others to believe and have hope is pathetic.

Consider the long-term effects of your personal walk with Jesus and ministry work. Be sure to weigh the risks and rewards associated with your decisions. Consider the ramifications of your actions and be sure the decisions you make are in line with God's Will. Yield and proceed with caution. "Wisdom comes with age; age does not come with wisdom." [SCR] Young people often miss their calling and don't know their worth and the value of their life. Some waste much of their youth. Ask yourself why you don't want to spend time with Jesus while you are young. Time is not something you can stop or get back. It's sad that grown-ups don't have time for kids and teens don't have time for grown-ups. Some people appear to be adulting with no skills. The body of Christ is a treasure trove untapped. Collectively, there is a wealth of knowledge and resources. *"Submit to one another out of reverence for Christ."* [Ephesians 5:21]

> *"Likewise, you who are younger, be subject to the elders. Clothe yourselves, all of you, with humility toward one another, for God opposes the proud but gives grace to the humble. Humble yourselves, therefore, under the mighty hand of God so that at the proper time he may exalt you, casting all your anxieties on him because he cares for you." [1 Peter 5:5-7]*

Yielding to God's perfect plan for your life and proceeding with caution as directed by Him is the way to escape a **toilet stool life.** It's a way to flush your spiritual plumbing system clean forever. Jesus said to you, *"I am the way, the truth, and the life. No one comes to the Father except through me"* [John 14:6] *"and you will know the truth, and the truth will set you free."* [John 8:32]

You should be jumping with joy right now. God, your Father, is living, and he's in the world today. You know He lives because he's in your heart. A true and living God who will never forsake you. I often think about times I was bullied because I was an "A" student. It didn't help by other people's account that I was a beautiful skinny tomboy with long hair. I knew Jesus at a young age. I didn't understand why I could see things before other people and before they happened. I didn't have church going parents, but I had parents who sent me and my siblings to church.

When we lived on 14th and Indiandale, in the city of Detroit, in a home said to be the former residence of the Black panthers, we could look out of our side window at the front door of the church next-door. Church happened every Sunday morning at our house whether my parents attended or not. We could hear the preaching and singing in our house. That is the only church that I recall in my childhood Big mama was not a member of. When we moved, we attended church where Big mama went. That was a whole unique experience. Big mama was an Usher on some Sundays and she sung in the Choir on others. We sat on the pews [my siblings and cousins] like ducks in a row. Big mama did not allow chewing gum, eating candy, talking, or any shenanigans in church. It didn't matter where Big mama was serving in the church, she watched us like a hawk. It was nothing for her to walk down out of the choir stand, index finger up, to where we were sitting, ball her fist up and connect her knuckles to the head of the disobedient culprit. I loved to see Big mama working in the church. She was a beacon light for Christ to her grandchildren—even though I didn't think she liked me.

One thing I learned to grow up is the realness of God. How faithful God was, is, and will be to his children. There is no more time to waste. If you don't know the love of Jesus, the Christ, our Lord, and Savior you are not living your life with any insurance or protection for eternal life. I strongly urge you to get a guaranteed for life insurance policy to live eternally saved at no cost. *"My God will supply every need of yours according to his riches in glory in Christ Jesus."* [Philippians 4:19] If you don't have a Big mama, Nana, GiGi, G-ma, Ma-dear, Glam-ma, Obaasan, Dada, Poppa, or Papa, that you can go to for spiritual support and guidance, build a strong relationship with your pastor or mentor(s) they can provide invaluable help and support. Engaging in Bible study and attending Sunday services will also provide spiritual guidance and inspiration. Don't forget to yield when God says yield and proceed with caution when He directs you.

CHAPTER 12

SPEED LIMIT 2 **SPEED LIMIT 3** **SPEED LIMIT 5** **SPEED LIMIT 15** **SPEED LIMIT 55** **SPEED LIMIT 75**

How Fast Should You Go?

How long does it take you to go when God says go? Do you ask yourself, was God really speaking to me? Do you ask other people what God meant when he told you to go? Do you wait for further instructions from God? Are you waiting for God to tell you when and where to go? Are you planning, organizing, what, when, where, and how? Do the answers to any of these posed questions depend on how fast God wants to you to go? Do you prepare to be ready but just don't feel you are ready to move because there is so much for you to do before you go? I know it sounds like you are going around and around the merry-go-round with this line of questions.

The fact is, you may spend a lot of time in preparation waiting for the opportunity to get your feet wet, but you don't always know what God wants you to do. Consider this scenario: You asked God [sometimes told God] you wanted a new job. One that would pay you more money and give more job security. That's it. You do nothing else. You wait at your old job-hoping God will come through for you. In the meantime, you prepare your resume and send it out while you are at work. You stop doing everything required of you on your current job because your plan is to get a new one. You send resumes out and you wait. Then you hear a voice saying Go! Your response, "I can't leave this job until I find a new one. I have bills to pay." You then question what you heard, and you do nothing. You fall into the abyss of nothingness. If something good happens, [you get a new job that pays more] you roll with it. Something bad occurs [you get fired] you grow angry with God.

To move when God says move requires attentive and active listening. The speed you should go depends on God's instructions. Therefore, faith is imperative. Without faith, you lack Trust. The reality is you lack confidence[faith] in yourself and don't trust yourself and you treat God in the same manner you treat yourself. You impose your limitations on God.

There is something to be learned by looking at the analogous speed limits on our roads. The lowest speed limit on many roads is typically 2 mph, a snail's pace. How often do we move at this speed when God says to move? Probably never. This is more like when God tells you to "Wait"– the words often come with a sense of stillness and patience. Similarly, a speed limit of 3 mph is still rather slow. This is when God is telling you to be careful, to think before you act, and to take heed of what you're doing. A speed limit of 5 mph a low average "get around" speed. You should consider the conditions of the terrain and the area, but it's still a respectable, middle-of-the-road speed. This is when God tells you to move, but not too quickly. A speed limit of 15 mph is a much faster pace. Consider the risks and be sure to be extra cautious when complying with God's commands. This is when God is telling you to move, but not to rush.

At, 55 mph and 75 mph you're picking up speed. At this limit, maintain alertness and presence of mind, as the consequences of not doing so could be catastrophic. This is when God says to move swiftly. God's instruction to you to "move" is unique to each individual situation. However, it's comforting to look at the speed limits in our everyday life as a reminder of what speed to strive for when God says to go or move.

When faced with a difficult situation, it's hard to know the right speed to move forward. To some, the impulse can be to rush ahead, but to others, the thought of moving fast can be overwhelming. In these times, it's helpful to look to God for guidance on the speed at which to move. Let me digress to say this, communicate with God daily. When you disconnect from God, it feels like playing catch up…like you are out-of-order trying to get fixed and reconnected. If you stay in God's presence daily and talk with Him, you stay linked. The Bible offers many reminders and encouragements to wait on the Lord and to trust in His plan. Proverbs 3:5-6 instructs you to, *"Trust in the Lord with all your heart and lean not on your own understanding; in all your ways acknowledge Him and He will make your paths straight."* If you can learn to trust in God's plan, you will be comfortable with the speed He chooses for you to go.

God's plan is perfect, and includes the timing of His Will. Psalm 37:23-24 explains this, *"The steps of a man are established by the Lord, when he delights in his way; though he falls, he shall not be cast headlong, for the Lord upholds his hand."* With the assurance of God's love and care, you can be confident with His guidance and how fast God wants you to move. When you face not knowing how fast to move, you can take comfort knowing God has already set a speed limit for you. He wants you to move at a pace that is comfortable and in harmony with His Will for your life. Moving at God's speed will ultimately bring you to the place where he wants you to be.

God's speed is not always about being fast or slow but about taking the time to properly assess your situation and making decisions that will bring about the best for your life. It is about making thoughtful decisions to honor God and working to make your step-by-step actions align with His plan. Ultimately, it is about trusting God. When considering the question of how fast to move, keep this truth in mind: There is no one-size-fits-all answer how fast one should move in life. Instead, trust in the Lord and wait on his timing, and you will find the speed at which you should be moving. It is necessary to be aware of yourself and those around you. Take the time to think about what holds you back from reaching your goals. Take a moment to reflect on your current circumstances and if any of them may be affecting the speed at which you're moving in life. Examine why you are feeling stressed and overwhelmed.

Look at responsibilities you have that take precedence over what you want to achieve? Pinpoint the sources of stress and chaos in your life. This will help you gain a better understanding of how to move in a manner that works for you. It is also important to remember to prioritize your wellbeing. Moving too quickly can lead to burnout, and it is important to pace yourself in order to stay balanced and healthy. Recognize when it is time to take a break, and be sure to do something that will help you relax and give your mind and body the reprieve they need. Ensure that a supportive network of family and friends surround you. Having a support system of people to help and encourage you is invaluable, and can often help make finding the right speed limit seem easier. Overall, remember to trust in the Lord and be true to yourself and those around you, and you will find the right pace for your life.

CHAPTER 13

Maintain Top Safe Speed is for successful spiritual growth and development. When you face difficult times, you must stay the course and remain firm in your beliefs and convictions. This way your efforts and labor will not be in vain. The Apostle Paul gave an important reminder when he penned 1 Corinthians 15:58: *"Therefore, my beloved brethren, be ye steadfast, unmovable, always abounding in the work of the Lord, forasmuch as ye know that your labor is not in vain in the Lord."* This means you must remain steadfast in your belief and not be easily swayed by others. You must not allow yourself to become sidetracked. This will prevent you from accomplishing the tasks set before you. At the same time, remember to pace yourself and don't push yourself too hard, you don't want to suffer from burnout or disillusionment.

When juggling both your personal and professional life, you must get the balance right to ensure you do not overwork yourself. Over working yourself can hinder you. The best way to ensure you get this balance right is to maintain Top Safe Speed. This means pacing yourself and not pushing yourself too hard. Stay the course and stay focused on the tasks before you. Remain sincere, humble, and open-minded as you go about fulfilling your duties. You will accomplish success and rid yourself from a toilet stool life nightmare.

Maintaining top safe speed on the highway is essential for any believer. It's a challenge to keep up with worshipping and spreading the good news while tackling chores and other responsibilities related to your job. It is easy to become distracted while driving on life's straight and narrow path especially if you are dealing with long stretches of road [issues] that lack any major landmarks or signs to let you know you are almost there. As a driver, it is necessary to remain aware of the speed limit and any restrictions in the area. Slowing down in congested areas and avoiding driving while distracted are ways to keep safe on the road.

Knowing the route and the speed limits along the way helps to ensure you are adhering to the posted speed limits. You should check the weather, traffic, and vehicle restrictions ahead of time to plan accordingly. Remember to take regular breaks. Rest stops allow you to refresh and recharge, making it easier to maintain your speed. Also, be aware of your physical limits to avoid drowsiness or fatigue that leads to decreased concentration. Apply everything just said to your off the road life.

There may be times you push yourself to move faster to remain on schedule. Stay within the legal speed limit and obey safety regulations. Safety comes first, and it should be your number one priority when driving and navigating through life's obstacles. Remain humble and open-minded about your capabilities and get to your destination in a safe manner.

A distance runner learns the terrain and develops his or her strategy to win the race. How fast they run determines whether they will win or not. The runner understands running at top speed throughout the entire 5K race is ludicrous and not possible. They must pace themselves and maintain the top speed for their pace to achieve the desired results they want. They learn their body when to push when to maintain a certain pace and speed and when to dig deep within themselves to run faster than they have ever run before. They run to win! Winning may be simply running their personal best time. Pastors may learn a thing or two from a distance runner. The Pastor runs a race of obedience to God. Self-sacrifice and a lifelong commitment to spreading the gospel beyond city limits to people some preachers would ignore. Did we say that out loud? Let's deal with the comment—some mega churches only want working members prayerfully affluent ones with large bank accounts. They depend on these parishioners to bring their tithes and offerings to the church. The needy people, unemployed, and the like who don't have the financial resources to bring to the church may belooked upon as members who drain the church benevolent funds if the church is not careful. The small church often gives to those in need and strive to meet the needs of the people in the community where they reside. They don't have a lot of money, but they pour whatever they have into the community and strive to nurture and build up the members of their local church. Our church has been very blessed to have mega churches come along side our Pastor's vision to ensure that everyone, no matter who they are and where they can experience the love of God. We are blessed to have a spiritual leader who thinks outside of the box and does not limit who God is. He inspires every single church attender and member to walk in their calling. He doesn't let these words fall from his lips without expectation God will do the rest.

He makes room in the church for people to step up, to grow, to dream, to live a life of obedience abundantly and he doesn't do it by taking up more than one offering. He doesn't teach people to steal from or cheat God. Let me explain this comment. I grew up in a church where the Pastor would have multiple offerings. He had a calculator in front of the church. When an offering was collected, he would tabulate it and say, "We need 10 people to give 100 dollars or more, and whoever loves God to give twenty or more and on down the line he'd go.

I learned from reading the Word of God at a young age we should give God our best gifts at all times Remember Cain and Abel? I learned people should come to church prepared with the gift they want to bless God with. Not the Church, God. When you give, you are giving to God to further God's kingdom. His ministry. You are supposed to provide financial support and sustenance to the man or woman of God He has sent to shepherd you. You should not get caught up in where the money is going if you are giving your tithes and offerings God asked you to give. Here's how some churches teach members to cheat or lie. If you attend a church where multiple offerings are taken up, and your prepared gift is 100 dollars–your tithe, than that's what you prepared to give. What I witnessed as a child and was somewhat coached to do, was to take my three dollars I was prepared to give and break it up over the 3 offerings. Some people did this to be seen giving in all offerings [this is when people got up and walked around the altar to place their tithes and offerings in the collection plate. I used to think of it as a fashion show "Sista's were dressed to the hilt to walk around or should I say prance for each of the offerings. What I am trying to say was the church in most cases, only got the same dollar amount the person intended to give spread out over the multiple collections.

The Pastor at my childhood church, would publish in the church bulletin the names of people who gave and how much they gave. He also utilized the church enclosed glass bulletin board to put up the bounced checks people gave for everyone to see. He'd stand in the pulpit and tell them to be sure to make their checks good at the end of the service. We may have laughed a bit as children, but I was always embarrassed for the people who were shamed in this way. To me, it made sense to just take up one offering to keep people honest about their prepared gift. Some Pastors may be able to shake a few extra dollars out here and there guilting people but I discovered from someone they only bring to church what they prepared to give and left their wallets and checkbooks at home so they could honestly say they gave all they prepared/had to give in the offering that day.

Pastors committed to God must maintain safely the vision and course God has for the church God called them to lead. Not all Pastors are the same and some get lost in seeking self-gain, fame, and notoriety [a small percentage of them]. They are human just as we are and can fall short by distractions. If the Pastor fails to maintain top speed as God directed, he can lose his way and struggle with anxiety and stress. Some Pastors may not be people persons because they struggle with rejection and let down. They know all too well how people can love you and follow you today and abandon and hate you tomorrow. They also know there are certain people who think Pastors should live in poverty, not have nice homes, and drive expensive cars. They hate on the men and women of God who are truly doing the right thing because they have seen to many Pastors in their opinion doing the wrong thing.

The body of Christ has many members with different talents and spiritual gifts and the house of God should have a full body operating in the ministry: Not two heads and two tails. Not two mouths and four eyes, and four ears. The body is one and on one accord. Hear what God has for you to do within the body of Christ and maintain top speed in serving Him and only Him! It's not about you. It's about giving God the Glory!

CHAPTER 14

TWO WAY TRAFFIC

The two-way traffic sign is a gift from God's warning toolbox. Relationships require two-way communication. God wants you to recognize communication and relationships are like a two-way street. Stay in your lane, respect the opposing views and opinions of others when you engage in two-way communication. Communication is key to healthy striving relationships. You should not make the eyes more important than the ears, or run through conversations like you are on a one-way street. God challenges you to use your ears more than you use your mouth. If you neglect this warning sign and cannot develop two-way communication with God and others, you're in danger of crashing and burning out your engine. Only God can give eternal blessings to you. An effective ministry provides opportunity for others to meet Christ and grow in His Word.

God's warning signs guide and protect you. When you hear other people's opinions, even if they don't align with yours you need to be open-minded. Also give the same respect to those whose views differ from yours. When it comes to the spiritual life, the two-way traffic sign is an invaluable warning. Building a relationship with God and knowing His word is the only way to gain full understanding of His love and grace.

Pass God's message on to others. Gain insight and develop a relationship with people you don't know. *"it is easy to love those who love you—even a tax collector can love those who love him. And it is easy to greet your friends—even outsiders do that! But you are called to something higher: 'Be perfect, as your Father in heaven is perfect."* [Matthew 5:46-48] You develop a genuine relationship when you listen to other people's stories, empathize with their struggles, and share your own experiences. People you consider undesirable, those who have an attitude problem along with a personality only their mother would love need friends too. Matthew 5:43-48 emphasizes this point:

> *"You have heard that it was said, 'You shall love your neighbor and hate your enemy.' But I say to you, Love your enemies and pray for those who persecute you, so that you may be sons of your Father who is in heaven. For he makes his sun rise on the evil and on the good, and sends rain on the just and on the unjust. For if you love those who love you, what reward do you have? Do not even the tax collectors do the same? And if you greet only your brothers, what more are you doing than others? Do not even the Gentiles do the same?"*

This passage of scripture definitely requires a long talk with God. This is a huge expectation. No one wants to be around people who manipulate and use them for their own personal gain. You might know some people who are always being slick and devising ways to get over on people. And you are expected to love them and pray for them. They wish! Pray to God for understanding. This two-way conversation with God allows you to approach the relationship cautiously while exercising a leap of faith. Pray for those who persecute you? Is this a mistake? What is God thinking? Those are questions you can ask if you don't understand the part that there is no reward attached to loving those who love you. The challenge is going after the undesirables you don't consider friends and reach out to them. Share God's love with them. Are you up for the challenge? No need to be fake about it. Smiling in peoples' face that you really don't like. That's not what God is asking you to do.

Always strive to find common ground and be open to learning from one another. Being in right relationship with people you know positions you to have meaningful conversations and opens an opportunity for you to share the good news about salvation. You received the gift of salvation at no cost. You should be eager to follow God's instruction: *"This is my commandment, that you love one another as I have loved you."* John 13:34-35: "A *new commandment I give to you, that you love one another: just as I have loved you, you also are to love one another. By this all people will know that you are my disciples, if you have love for one another."* There is a reason this commandment is repeated more than once. This world that pits people against one another, two-way traffic-communication helps to bridge the gap of understanding. When you listen and hear what someone else is saying, you are validating their worth and ability to express themselves. You don't have to agree with what they are saying. You are showing them respect even if their views oppose yours. Here's something to think about: You want people to listen to you and respect you right? With God's help you can foster a sense of community and build meaningful relationships with one another. No, you don't have to change your opinion or your ways to accommodate someone else's perspective.

I found one final scripture to share about loving one another in 1 John 4:7-21

> *Beloved, let us love one another, for love is from God, and whoever loves has been born of God and knows God. Anyone who does not love does not know God, because God is love. In this the love of God was made manifest among us, that God sent his only Son into the world, so that we might live through him. In this is love, not that we have loved God but that he loved us and sent his Son to be the propitiation for our sins. Beloved, if God so loved us, we also ought to love one another.*

Remain compassionate while having the courage to stand firm in your faith. The two-way traffic sign likened to two-way communication will make a big difference in your life and those around you. Because you can listen and empathize with others while allowing them to truly hear and understand you. The beauty of two-way communication is it goes beyond just being an effective way to communicate, it's an important component of having meaningful relationships. You are being open to the views an opinions of others. Create an environment that fosters mutual respect and understanding. You open yourself to new experiences and perspectives and you embrace diversity and beauty life offers. Again, have the courage to stand firm in your faith and belief, even when your belief is unpopular.

This courage is necessary for you to be open and honest about your belief without worrying about how others will perceive you. It helps to stay true to our own conscience, which can be a firm foundation for the relationships you build. Two-way traffic helps to create an atmosphere of balance, where you are comfortable with yourself with the people in your life. In a world full of intolerance and misunderstanding, two-way communication is key.

It is increasingly challenging to form meaningful two-way relationships, especially with God. A relationship with God is an integral part of living a fulfilled and meaningful life. A two-way relationship with our loving God is a blessing. You can benefit from the spiritual, emotional, and physical guidance He provides you and you will know His Will and plan for your life.

This means creating an environment that is conducive to both parties being able to communicate with one another in a non-judgmental manner. Two-way conversations should be built on mutual respect, trust, and understanding. Having a two-way relationship with others can also provide spiritual, emotional, and physical healing. You can learn to be patient, and more understanding of one another.

Examples of two-way relationships can be found throughout the Bible. One example is the relationship between Moses and God. God sent Moses to lead the Israelites out of Egypt. Moses had to have conversations with God to learn His plan and instructions on how to lead the Israelites out. Jesus, spoke with God. Jesus' life was framed in a two-way dialogue with God. Though Jesus was divine, he was born fully human. He used his two-way relationship with God to provide healing, guidance, and wisdom to the surrounding people.

In conclusion, having a two-way relationship with God and with others is essential for developing a meaningful and fulfilling life. Building a two-way relationship with God is one of the most rewarding experiences in life. Through prayer and study of Scripture, we open ourselves up to God's direction and guidance. When you take the time to cultivate a relationship with God, through prayer and spending time in God's Word, you experience God's power in your life.

Every relationship needs patience; it takes time to build trust, foster communication, and learn one another's needs. As we communicate with God through prayer, we need to be patient and understanding of God's answers, even when they don't come as quickly or in the way we expect. Love is the key ingredient for any relationship. Show God your love by respecting His position and authority, being humble, and committing to Him. As you grow closer to God, your love for Him will increase and deepen your spiritual bond. A relationship with God is a beautiful and powerful experience that provides you with the assurance of His perpetual love and guidance. When you seek God in your time of need, you will learn to practice love, patience, and mercy.

The first step in developing a two-way relationship with God is to develop an understanding of who He is. God is a loving and compassionate Father who loves you unconditionally. He is also an all-powerful being who watches over you and guides you. God listens to your prayers and answers them in His own way, sometimes in unexpected or surprising ways. He also provides you with the strength and courage you need to face difficult circumstances. As you learn to trust in God's goodness and wisdom, you will feel secure. You know God will always be with you, no matter what challenges or struggles you face.

The second step in developing a two-way relationship with God is to open your heart and mind to Him. This means you must let go of your own agenda and opinion for His. That's another book!

CHAPTER 15

STAY
IN
LANE

Have you ever heard someone tell you to "Stay in your Lane?" This phrase is used in many settings: driving, ministry work, and in everyday conversations. Staying in your lane is an important concept for Christians to remember and can be found in many Bible verses. It means you should focus on your life and not get distracted by things not related to what God has called you to do. It involves living according to His will and not allowing yourself to be swayed by the world's values and desires.

This is not an elementary concept to grasp, but it is one of the many ways you can honor God and bring Him glory. The Bible gives insight into how you should live in order to stay in your lane. In Romans 12:2 it says, *"Do not be conformed to this world, but be transformed by the renewal of your mind, that by testing you may discern what is the will of God, what is acceptable and perfect."* This should remind you to focus your life on pleasing God rather than pleasing the world. You should strive to seek His will and live accordingly. Another passage that speaks to this idea is 1 Timothy 6:12 which says, *"Fight the good fight of faith, lay hold of eternal life, to which you were also called and have confessed the good confession in the presence of many witnesses."* This reminds you to live out your faith and not let it become something that you give up on. You should have confidence in God's plan for you and strive to seek it out. Finally, Philippians 4:13 encourages you to remain focused on the tasks God has set before you. It says, *"I can do all things through Him who strengthens me."* This is a reminder to trust God's strength and to depend on Him in all of your endeavors. Staying in your lane is an important concept for Christians to remember. It involves focusing on your life and living out God's will. The Bible gives insight into how to do this by reminding you to not be conformed to this world, to fight the good fight of faith, and to rely on His strength. As you remember these verses, be encouraged to stay in your lane and discover God's purpose for your life. Another example of staying in your lane is referenced in Psalm 1:1-6:

> *Blessed is the man who walks not in the counsel of the wicked, nor stands in the way of sinners, nor sits in the seat of scoffers; but his delight is in the law of the Lord, and on his law, he meditates day and night. He is like a tree planted by streams of water that yields its fruit in its season, and its leaf does not wither. In all that he does, he prospers. The wicked are not so, but are like chaff that the wind drives away. Therefore, the wicked will not stand in the judgment, nor sinners in the congregation of the righteous; ...*

This passage of scripture is one that you should learn by heart. It is packed with warnings you should heed. You live in a society where people counsel one another most times with no expertise on the subject matter. They are usually interpreting a one-sided situation you shared with them, and the advice rolls easily off their tongues. It sounds something like: "If I were you, I would…"

If you avoid walking in the counsel of wicked people and stay out of the sinner's way, you can avoid a tumultuous traffic jam when you stay in your lane of meditating day and night on God's Word. You will prosper in everything you do! You are probably wondering why you haven't prospered yet. Good Question. The only answer I can offer is maybe you haven't been doing what this passage of scripture says and have found yourself wrapped up in a toilet stool life with no way of flushing it. Maybe you have been lane hopping in search for opportunity and recognition. Only you can truthfully answer this question.

God commands you to stay in the lane of Love. That means you have to exchange all the hate and bitterness you hold in your heart towards others for love. Don't let negative people A.K.A. "haters" interfere with what God expects of you:

> *If I speak in the tongues of men and of angels, but have not loved, I am a noisy gong or a clanging cymbal. And if I have prophetic powers, and understand all mysteries and all knowledge, and if I have all faith, to remove mountains, but have not love, I am nothing. If I give away all I have, and if I deliver up my body to be burned, but have not love, I gain nothing. Love is patient and kind; love does*

not envy or boast; it is not arrogant or rude. It does not insist on its own way; it is not irritable or resentful; ... [1 Corinthians 13:1-13]

It may be hard to avoid people who rub you the wrong way, but you must remain steadfast in your lane that yields prosperity for you as you delight in the knowledge of God's Word. Take an example here from Apostle Paul:

"I, Paul, myself entreat you, by the meekness and gentleness of Christ—I who am humble when face to face with you, but bold toward you when I am away! — I beg of you that when I am present, I may not have to show boldness with such confidence as I count on showing against some who suspect us of walking according to the flesh. For though we walk in the flesh, we are not waging war according to the flesh. For the weapons of our warfare are not of the flesh but have divine power to destroy strongholds. We destroy arguments and every lofty opinion raised against the knowledge of God, and take every thought captive to obey Christ, ..." [2 Corinthians 10:1-18]

If you know anything about Apostle Paul, you know that there is nothing in his character that suggest that he is wimpy or afraid. He was a true hater of Christians. He hunted them down and persecuted them during a phase of his life where he lacked knowledge. God met him on the road to Damascus where Paul's eyesight was temporarily taken. Paul's transformation and understanding of God, lived out in his Son, Jesus, the Christ brought Paul to the true understanding of who he is in Christ. You may have a few hiccups in your past you are not proud of. Perhaps you provided false counsel to some people because you told them what they wanted to hear and not the truth. Maybe this is how you rolled:

"Whoever isolates himself seeks his own desire; he breaks out against all sound judgment. A fool takes no pleasure in understanding, but only in expressing his opinion. When wickedness comes, contempt comes also, and with dishonor comes disgrace. The words of a man's mouth are deep waters; the fountain of wisdom is a bubbling brook. It is not good to be partial to the wicked or to deprive the righteous of justice" [Proverbs 18: 1-24.]

Maybe during this time in your life, you weren't in your lane, meditating day, and night on God's plan for you in His Word. Trust God when he says it's not too late for you to get with the program… get back into your lane. This may require you to let some people and things go from your life. You don't have to have a long-drawn-out pity party about it either. Just do it!

In case you have not put two and two together yet, the Stay in Lane warning sign can interact with the two-way traffic sign. The two-way traffic sign helps you understand the importance of staying in your lane, because you know the lanes are moving in two different directions. Accidents can happen if you cross over at the wrong time going in the wrong direction. The two-way traffic sign also shows you when it's safe to change lanes to go in a different direction, and move forward. Waiting patiently on God and communicating with God is the glue that keeps you knitted together. So, how does this play out in ministry work?

For ministry work, people may caution others to "stay in their lane." Most times, they mean pastors should be pastors, and they shouldn't try to do something they are not called to do. Unfortunately, there are also those who serve as "stay in lane cops" lurking around in many churches, boardrooms, parties, and community organizations. They zap people with their criticism and admonish them for serving. Be careful that this is not you. You don't know what God is calling other people to do unless they tell you and you certainly don't run or control God's church. Take heed to the lane you should stay in and not jump into the unauthorized judgment lane stated in Matthew 7: 1-29:

> *"Judge not, that you be not judged. For with the judgment, you pronounce you will be judged, and with the measure you use it will be measured to you. Why do you see the speck that is in your brother's eye, but do not notice the log that is in your own eye? Or how can you say to your brother, 'Let me take the speck out of your eye,' when there is the log in your own eye? You hypocrite, first take the log out of your own eye, and then you will see clearly to take the speck out of your brother's eye. ..."*

It is hard for multi-gifted, multi-taskers, visionaries, administrators, and creative people to stay in the lane, that "stay in your lane cops" try to impose on them while the cops get their hands involved and take control of the project. Not sure if you have encountered a person who assigns a task to you only to insist or make you do it their way. They go behind your back sowing seeds of discourse, they talk about the poor job you are doing, they email people behind your back and position people to do their biddings at the expense of your reputation and feelings. They don't trust anyone can do anything better than them including the preacher. Yes, there are people in church who want to control what the preacher can preach about and how the message is delivered. The same individuals think they know more than their supervisors or boss and always have something to say about everything. It's only good when they do it. That is why organizations, corporate and non-profits only have a faithful few to do all the work. These are the few who probably communicate with God daily, meditate on the Word, and do not let people be the boss of them! Perhaps they understood 2 Corinthians 4:1-18:

> *"Therefore, having this ministry by the mercy of God, we do not lose heart. But we have renounced disgraceful, underhanded ways. We refuse to practice cunning or to tamper with God's word, but by the open statement of the truth we would commend ourselves to everyone's conscience in the sight of God. And even if our gospel is veiled, it is veiled to those who are perishing. In their case the god of this world has blinded the minds of the unbelievers, to keep them from seeing the light of the gospel of the glory of Christ, who is the image of God.*

For what we proclaim is not ourselves, but Jesus Christ
as Lord, with ourselves as your servants for Jesus' sake"

You must stay focused on who you are and what you believe. Staying in your lane from a spiritual growth standpoint does not mean you are stuck forever in one place or position. In fact, it is an invitation for you to get ready for what He has planned for you next. God does not ask you to do something you are not equipped to do. This is the time to focus on your own goals and dreams without having to pivot to do something someone wants you to do that is not in your lane. Staying in your lane keeps you true to your personal goals and aspirations that align with your spiritual gift(s). The thoughts and actions of those around you does not distract you. It is important to have people in your life who support your dreams and provide a much-needed boost of encouragement, motivation, and support but do not get caught up in comparison or competition with those around you. For those who like to micro-manage everything – expect nothing in return for all your efforts, aside from stress and disappointment.

God's plans for you are unique and you will know you are headed in the right direction. You can trust God's plan. It will benefit you. God knows what's best for you. You need to trust His guidance and never succumb to efforts designed to pull you away from God. The next time you feel overwhelmed by the ideas and plans of those around you, Say "NO." Remember to *"seek the Lord and his strength; seek his presence continually!"* [Psalm 105:4]

No one else can fulfill the unique call God has for you. It's easy to get discouraged when you think you are falling behind compared to others. God is always with you on your journey. When you follow

God's plan, you are exactly where you need to be. Don't allow yourself to be sucked into comparisons and distractions from others. Remember, God's mercy endures forever and His plan for you is perfect!

CHAPTER 16

When you observe a traffic sign, "Pass with Care," you should take extra caution when passing by pedestrians, non-believers, bikers, and vehicles. To pass with care requires you to be alert, take your time, and make sure everyone is safe from potential danger. This means you should not be texting messages while you are driving or riding a bike.

When God says, "Pass with Care," it means to take extra precaution when you interact with people around you. It may be difficult to be around people from different backgrounds. You may not know how to respond to homeless individuals, people with mental health issues, or children in foster care. In these circumstances, God called you to be kind, and understanding, while respecting boundaries. You can care for people in need without becoming overly involved in their lives or judging them. Passing with care requires you to resist the urge to act with your emotions. You must act based on love and wisdom from God.

When you do not think before you act, you may cause more harm than good. Therefore, take time to be still, listen to God's voice, and pass with care. Passing with care requires you to be thoughtful it is not just about understanding the consequences of your decisions, but also about understanding what God wants from you.

When you listen to God's voice, you gain perspective on what you need to do to make wise and responsible decisions. You should think about what you do and how you go about it. He wants you to have the strength and courage to stand up for what is right. For instance, if you decide you want to help homeless people, first don't assume they want your help, or should I say the type of help you want to impose upon them. Calling the police to make them move off the street from your perspective might get them the help they need but they may consider your kind of help an intrusive nightmare. While you thought a night in a warm jail cell might be better than sleeping on the cold streets, they may disagree.

You may be a person who speaks rudely to a person who approaches you begging for money. You might give them a tongue lashing about responsibility and finding a job while tossing them a quarter that won't help them. Be careful, God warns you: "*Whoever oppresses a poor man insults his maker, but he who is generous to the needy honors him.*" [Proverbs 14:31] Why throw a bone to a hungry person with no meat? The person is a human being, and you don't know their story. You don't know their why? Yet you draw conclusions and assumptions from your limited knowledge base. Why not invest in your local shelters or partner with community leaders to establish affordable housing so everyone can live with dignity and respect. How about volunteering at your local food bank or soup kitchens? This may give you a bird's-eye view in the world of people you are trying to help not hinder. I recall lyrics to a song that said something like "if you can't help me, move out of my way..."

To pass with care involves looking for the best and right way to act in any situation. You need to be aware of the potential impact of your choices and decisions. Passing with care is about being intentional and deliberate with your actions. Learn the facts and then determine the best course of action. You must sacrifice your own interests and put the interests of others first. When you try to manipulate opportunities to serve so you get recognition for it you already have your reward. It's sad to take advantage of people and use them to better your position. If you are only volunteering so you can have table conversation about the poor and unfortunate helpless people, you need to get a God-fearing life!

Proverbs 19:17 states, *"Whoever is generous to the poor lends to the Lord, and he will repay him for his deed."* When you have the right heart about what you do and your intention is to glorify God-not yourself, you would rather for God to repay you for your deed rather than man. Recently, our President with the help of those who supported the effort, canceled student loan debts of students lifting a heavy burden off of many who had been carrying the burdensome debt for over ten-years not able to see how they could ever pay the debt over their lifetime. They spent millions if not billions of dollars forgiving these debts. Personally, I never imagined the government doing anything like this for anyone. I never saw this coming. I never thought some people would be upset they paid their student loans without government relief while others got a huge break. But we jump to assumptions and conclusions without knowing the forgiven stories. That is why God is God! God looks upon a person's bountiful eye. He says that person will be blessed because he shares his bread with the poor. [Proverbs 22:9]

I can surely attest to this promise. Instead of being mad, jealous, or envious, like Cain was, pay attention to scriptures that tell you how to please God. Deuteronomy 15:11, *"For there will never cease to be poor in the land. Therefore, I command you, 'You shall open wide your hand to your brother, to the needy and to the poor, in your land."* This requires you to go beyond your own understanding and trust God has your best interests in mind. If you give to the poor, God said you will not want. This means God will meet all of your needs. But if you hide your eyes [try to act like you don't see the homeless person or the woman begging for money for food], you will get many a curse. [Proverbs 28:27] You are supposed to *"remember the poor, the very thing I was eager to do."* [Galatians 2:10] If you despise your neighbor, you are a sinner, but the one who is generous to the poor is blessed. [Proverbs 14:21]

Our brother, Apostle Paul, gives us yet another answer how to get blessed: *"In all things I have shown you that by working hard in this way we must help the weak and remember the words of the Lord Jesus, how he himself said, 'It is more blessed to give than receive."* Consider this helpful passage of scripture when you tire of seeing people outside of the grocery store, gas station, games, and restaurants begging for money. If you really want to make a difference, Plan to run into someone in need so you can bless them.

Passing with care is an act of obedience to God's will. You must pay attention to your conscience and be sure to live under God's commands. You must have an open heart and mind to respond to God's promptings and recognize the power of His Word. Stop being skeptical about everything. Listen and Learn! No one knows you better than God. To pass with care requires you to humble yourself enough to take responsibility for your mistakes and accept the consequences of your decisions, knowing God will guide you in the right direction.

Ultimately, passing with care involves listening to God's voice and following His lead. When you listen to your inner voice, and feel the peace that comes with His guidance, you will be sure that your decisions will lead to the best outcome.

As you pause, listen, and pass with care as God directs, you will be assured of the knowledge God loves you and will make a way for you to pass with care. If you want to go deeper in pleasing God and not your friends, fraternity, or sorority ponder Luke 12:33-34:

"Sell your possessions and give to the poor. Provide purses for yourselves that will not wear out, a treasure in heaven that will never fail, where no thief comes near, and no moth destroys. **For where your treasure is, there your heart will be as well**.*"* Where is your treasure? Honestly, I think it's where you spend your time and money. Time and money are valuable resources that should never be wasted or flaunted. How much time do you spend serving an organization other than your church and spend your money? Conferences, where you hobnob to jockey for position, status, and recognition. Practicing a crab in a barrow routine. Stepping on and over anyone and everyone you can for a title. If you ever heard the question "will a man rob God" the answer is **YES!** Man will do it all the time because he wants to be somebody who is reverenced and adored. It's sad when I see women and men who claim to know

God and serve Him, but put him on the back burner where God isn't a close second in their life.

Listening to people brag about the things they have done in an organization they feel qualifies them to lead and serve in leadership roles, or why they should be elected for office, when they have lost their husband, wife, children, to gain the position. Their definition of winning is, to lie to get what they want. Prey on the weak…the meek…Off with Their Heads and reputation if they have a competitive edge over you. Some stoop so low as to hide behind-the-scenes meetings engaging in conversation to sway people to do their biddings. How about sending emails out to a select few people asking them to show up at a meeting to make a motion that supports your personal micro-managing agenda? It's all about you and less about the people you serve. Have people grown so gullible that truth no longer matters? Integrity means nothing?

To hear God's voice, to hold on to God's unchanging hand, is the only way you can successfully "Pass by with Care." To pass with care is a vital part of life you practice. Not only does it ensure you make informed decisions, but it also reveals your trust in God. God will make a way for you to pass with care and lead you to the best possible outcome. Remember, God loves you and wants the best for you. Discuss your plans and strategy with God. God is the wisest counselor you will ever meet. Even if your decisions lead you down a crooked path, you can trust God will lead you to the best outcome in the end. Listen to God and allow Him to guide you.

When you pray and listen with an open heart, God provides you with strength and knowledge to pass with care. His love and guidance are always with you, even in the hardest moments, and He will never leave you alone.

"Pass Me Not Oh Gentle Savior"
Pass with Care

The Bible has many scriptures about the importance of compassion when helping others, and God's call for you to share the Good News of Salvation. You usually think of this as helping those who are close to you or meeting their immediate needs. But what about those moments when you "pass by" someone, such as a homeless person on the street? Are you called to "pass them with care" even then? When you encounter someone who is especially vulnerable, consider the traffic sign that reads "Pass with Care." This reminds you to use caution to give plenty of space and room to maneuver. In a spiritual sense, this sign can also represent how you should approach those who are in need. You should always pass with special care, ensuring you respect the individual and strive to serve them in a manner that honors their dignity and the Lord.

The Bible gives you several examples of this idea in action. One of the best-known stories is when Jesus passed by a crowd of people in need of healing and ministry—including those who were lame, blind, and leprous. As told in Matt. 9:35-36, Jesus was moved with compassion for the people and healed them and showed them mercy. In a similar way, God calls you to pass people and things with particular care. This means you should help those in need, even if they don't "look or smell right" in the eyes of the world. Also in Luke 10: 25-37, Jesus told a parable of the Good Samaritan. A traveler, assumed to be Jewish, who was stripped of his clothing and beaten. Two people with the opportunity to help him, a Jewish Priest and a Levite ignored him and passed by. They did not take care to see if he was dead or alive or in need of any help. They crossed the street. But a Samaritan who is not considered a friend, passed with care to where he stopped and did what he could to assist the man and care for his needs. He was genuine to the point that he sought to make sure the man had housing and food to eat in his absence. The message is love one another. How many times have you crossed the street to avoid people? How many times have you crossed the street and left the person for dead on the road? This could have been you. Thank God for this warning!

You should go to places that are not necessarily pleasant or comfortable, offering aid and support to those who are struggling just as Jesus did. Besides passing people with special care, you are called to let them know how they can be born again. This means you should share the Gospel with those who need to hear it and do your best to spread the love of Christ to those who are lost and seeking salvation. This is something Jesus insisted upon in his commission to the disciples in Matt. 28:19-20, urging them to *"Go therefore and make disciples of all nations, baptizing them in the name of the Father and of the Son and of the Holy Spirit."*

This is how you can truly pass with care, ensuring all can hear the Good News of salvation. The phrase *"Pass Me Not oh Gentle Savior"* serves as a reminder you should always strive to pass with special care, not just on the road, but in your life as well. It is difficult to pass by those who are suffering, but remember God calls you to pass with great care, providing aid and compassion to those in need and spreading the message of salvation to all.

Pass Me Not, Oh Gentle Savior in a world full of strife and suffering, it might be easy for you to pass by those who are struggling because you are busy with your own life, and you reason you don't have time to help someone going through a hard time. But, when you take a moment to pause and consider your faith, you find God calls you to do just that.

The Bible contains many passages that speak to this, but there is a powerful hymn "Pass Me Not, Oh Gentle Savior." Written by Fanny Crosby in 1868, this song describes the hope God will not pass by those in need of His mercy, grace, and love. The chorus of the hymn reads *"pass me not, oh gentle Savior, hear my humble cry; while on others Thou art calling, do not pass me by."* In this hymn, you learn God desires you to approach those in need of loving kindness and compassion. You must remember in your own busy life, there will always be someone out there that needs help.

Whether you provide food to the hungry, offer a kind word to the discouraged, or simply be present for those in pain, you can show God's love and compassion to those around you. "Pass me Not oh Gentle Savior" is a beautiful and poignant hymn that reminds and encourages you to be cognizant of the suffering and sorrow of others and to take action to help them in any way you can. The words of the hymn illustrate the importance of being a compassionate presence in the lives of those struggling with grief, loss, or hardship. This hymn urges you to serve to the extent your kindnesses and compassion reflects the love of God.

Keep in mind those struggling and reach out to them with love and understanding. Whether it be through words of comfort, gestures of care, or physical acts of help, you must show your willingness to show compassion to those in pain. Sometimes you are focused on helping people with food, clothing, and shelter you forget the most precious gift you can ever give them: **Jesus!** You must pass with great care and make sure you do not pass anyone by, so no one is left feeling alone or neglected.

While the lyrics "Pass me Not oh Gentle Savior" speaks volumes in the few short lines of the hymn, it is up to you to be mindful of its message and commit to showing care and concern to others whether it is at your home, work, school, or some social event. By placing your own needs to the side and being attentive to the needs and concerns of others you can build relationships that reflect the life of Jesus to others by your actions.

Think about the time you helped someone with paying their rent. How about the time you could have given someone a ride they desperately needed. How about the time you could have provided food, clothing, and shelter but you closed the door tired of people because you were down to your last dime, but God showed up and blessed you. Have you ever been down and out so much you needed God to make a significant impact in your life right now?

Let's establish helping others is not about you. It's not to give you brownie points or to give you something to brag about or toot your horn about. God wants you to have a pure heart. Be sincere about your motives and pass people with care in a manner God's love covers them with mercy and grace.

CHAPTER 17

No Passing Zone is a traffic sign that notifies drivers there is a section of the road where they may not overtake or pass another vehicle. But beyond the physical road, there is a spiritual No Passing Zone. We can equate this spiritual No Passing Zone to a warning from God to take care of the widows, poor, sick, and shut-in individuals. God's No Passing Zone is a sign to signal followers of Christ to not pass people in need of the Savior. All zones where impoverished people live should be a zone you don't pass up. Christians should not ignore this sign. You should take time to uplift and empower these individuals. In Matthew 25:40: *"The King will reply, Truly I tell you, whatever you did for one of the least of these brothers and sisters of mine, you did for me."*

People need to be heard and seen, not pitied, passed up, or looked down upon. God's mercy and grace continues to be abundant and can be seen in the good deeds said and done by those who take the No Passing Zone sign to heart. When driving, you must obey the No

Passing Zone sign, and the same is true for the spiritual No Passing Zone sign. Many lack financial means and resources and may need additional help. Get to know people, become involved with their life, and offer guidance and support if they will allow it. Get them motivated to get out of the No Passing Zone into a place of faith. Make the time and effort to help others receive the message of salvation Jesus Christ freely gives to them. Jesus died for all, including those found in a place of poverty and despair. Help them out of the No Passing Zone and into a place of love and safety.

Though the physical road may not be the same, the path to grace remains the same. In our ever-changing world, be sure to remember God's instruction to take care of the widows, poor, sick, and shut in. Pay attention to the No Passing Zone sign, take it to mean you can't pass by people in a Zone God sends you to share the message of salvation with. Like you, they have ears to hear. God will inspire you to take the action. What if this sign was more than just a reminder to drive safely what if it was a message of hope and encouragement for those who are poor, sick, and shut in? God sends a powerful message we can all pay attention to.

God's Word gives you the motivation and courage to take action and to care for the vulnerable and marginalized in our society. We, as a society, can do our part to ensure those who are poor, sick, and shut in are not forgotten. You can advocate for their needs and ensure we hear their voices. You can provide necessities like food, medical care, and transportation. You can support organizations and programs that bring about social change and provide hope. Most of all, you can pray and trust God to provide for those in need.

The No Passing Zone is more than a warning to slow down; it signals you to pay attention to the needs of your neighbors and to be an active part of the caring and sharing community. This sign is a necessary safety feature for many physical and spiritual roads. It is important for drivers to be aware of the importance of these zones and how they should navigate through them. You will definitely avoid life's traffic jams when you obey God. Drivers should not attempt to pass other vehicles when driving in a No Passing Zone, as it can lead to serious accidents or fatalities. By respecting these No Passing Zones, drivers can help ensure the safety of those around them. This can be done by allowing them to get in front of you or finding a safe place to pull off to the side of the road. If a driver is stuck behind a slow-moving vehicle, he should wait for a safe spot to pass or follow them until it's safe to go around them.

In addition, drivers should remember "No Passing Zones" are there to protect pedestrians and cyclists. When driving in these designated areas, be sure to look out for any pedestrians or cyclists who may be present. Drive slowly and take your time when passing, it's dangerous to these vulnerable groups. This act of kindness is a much-needed reminder simple acts of caring will make a world of difference in someone's life.

CHAPTER 18

Hospitality Please

We often see church visitors as a blessing and a sign of God's grace. Providing a parking spot for visitors on church grounds and designating seats in the sanctuary for them is a warm and welcoming way to show the love of Christ. Some visitors seek answers, or look for a spiritual connection, an inviting sanctuary can be a great help as long as smiling faces and warm hearts welcomes them, showing them, they arrived at the right place. It's a great way to show hospitality and to provide a safe place for visitors to get to know Christ as their Lord and Savior. Hebrews 13:2: *"Do not forget to show hospitality to strangers, for by so doing some people have shown hospitality to angels without knowing it."* Can you imagine having an angel smack dab in the middle of your church service? What would you do differently if you could see an angel in human form?

Do you have an intentional strategy to make guest comfortable? Guests feel welcomed and loved when church members take the time to get to know them and to walk alongside them. By offering friendly conversation and listening to their story, [not being nosey and prying into their personal life] church members can show the love of Christ and create an environment that helps visitors feel accepted and supported. Churches can provide physical help by providing meals, access to resources, and support with physical, emotional, or spiritual needs of its members.

Skeptical people watch to see if you have a Sunday and a Monday face. Sometimes the only bible people will read is you. Hospitality and hospitable people can make a world of difference in church communities. People attach welcoming people, delightful music, and a friendly message to a pleasant experience. If they had a wonderful experience and those other factors lined up for them, they may visit again next time with some family members or friends.

Perhaps you host dinners, parties, or events at your home, and you want to make your guest feel welcome. Nowadays some host will provide valet parking for their guest. You do everything you can think of to make your guest feel welcomed and at home. The host in Genesis 24:31 greeted his guest in the following way: *"He said, Come in, O blessed of the Lord. Why do you stand outside? For I have prepared the house and a place for the camels."* You would feel welcomed, wouldn't you? This person even made provision for the camels which requires much more attention, provision, and care than a car.

I was a member of what some considered a very esteemed and reputable church. Many of the members of this church were affluent, and some were legacies of the founders of the church or grew up in the church. The church established a school on its campus and has a rectory of sorts where missionaries stay when they return from the mission fields. This church offered many bible study and fellowship opportunities. Some opened their homes to members for Bible study fellowships. The Pastor a very compassionate man of God shared a vision he had one January evening with the congregants. God revealed the church needed to extend its ministry to the community around the church. He mentioned the church was to cast a net throughout the local community and open the doors to those who would come. This vision was not an opportunity to go after new members, the church already had two services regularly filled. It was a staunch white congregation enjoyed by many of its congregants who wanted to keep it that way. There was a sprinkle here and there of people of color.

They cast the net into the community by mailing a video tape that shared the life of Jesus and his love and gift of salvation to all. In the meantime, in the sermon he talked about racism and God's command to love our brothers and sisters of color. I knew then he preached his last sermon at that church. He was a man who put God's instructions to him first. The next thing he did that probably caused some people to almost drop dead in their seats was he invited a well-known African American Choir to minister in song at the church. It was something this congregation did not know how to handle. In my few years of membership there, I never saw the people shout or worship, clap their hands, dance, or do anything that would suggest they were having a good time and enjoying the service. When I say they were staunch, they were clockwork staunch. Ceremonial and ritualistic staunch. It wasn't long before they tossed this Pastor out of the church. [I am sure they wouldn't put it this way] but it's what I recall. The one thing causing me to chuckle a bit resulted from casting the net out into the community surrounding the church. I am not sure how far out from the church the nets were cast by distribution of the Jesus video tapes, but one Sunday, for the first time in the history of that church in my humble opinion, I saw diversity in the halls of the church. More black and Asian people than I had ever seen while I attended the church. The Chuckle was a warm heart of seeing mixed couples along with their children. You might only understand my happy heart if you were there observing what God had done to honor the Pastor's act of obedience. It was a wonderment!

At the time I was a member, women could not teach men. It was frowned upon and for a long time not allowed. Of course, they vetted me through their new members class before I could venture to serve in any capacity. When I applied to fill a vacancy on its leadership team [can't remember if this is what it was called] they asked me questions about what my husband thought about me wanting to serve. It was a very intrusive beyond boundaries inquiry that let me know that the interview was really about the black man that wasn't there for the inquiring minds to ask him about his values, belief, leadership, and thoughts about whether he was giving me permission to serve in the role I sought. Without the answers to these inquiring minds—people want to know hidden questions; It was obvious I did not fit in. They had a culture of hiring or selecting wives of the men who served in leadership and teaching roles. [White men and women] My husband was not a member of this church. He continued to serve in his role as deacon at a Baptist church in Detroit where I later joined him as a member. [that is another conversation.]

If you are a member of a church like this one, and you believe you are serving God by shunning his children, your brothers, and sisters in Christ just because their skin color differs from yours or their socio-economic status is not to your liking, I suggest you pray and ask God to forgive you for your haughty and prideful heart. How can you truly be hospitable men and women of God when you have members in your congregation who support the ministry with their time, talent, and resources you don't want to sit next to? You don't want them to teach your children. The only capacity you would allow them to serve is a janitorial position to clean your church and school. That's truly the only job I recall seeing a black man or person working in at that church and its school.

I don't understand the biblical reasoning of believers in staunch church environments black or white that worship like there are two separate Heavens: one for whites and another for everybody else [I pray that sharing my experience is an eye opener that challenges us to examine ourselves]. I am going to guess they are okay with there being one Hell. "Oh, children of Adam and Eve. Look how stuck we are. No actual progress in understanding what unconditional true love is about. Not understanding what it really means to love our neighbors like we love ourselves." Church is not designed to be ["separate but not equal."]

We see the great invitation extended by God in Isaiah 55:1-9

"Ho, EVERYONE that thirst-eth, come ye to the waters, and he hath no money; come ye, buy, and eat; yea, come, buy wine and milk without money and without price. Wherefore do ye spend money for that which

is not bread? And your labour for that which satisfieth not? Hearken diligently unto me, and eat ye that which is good, and let your soul delight itself in fatness. Incline your ear, and come unto me: hear, and your soul shall live; and I will make an everlasting covenant with you, even the sure mercies of David. Behold, I have given him for a witness to the people, a leader and commander to the people. Behold thou shalt call a nation that thou knoweth not, and nations that knew not thee shall run unto thee because of the Lord thy God, and for the Holy One of Israel: for he hath glorified thee. Seek ye the Lord while he may be found, call ye upon him while he is near: Let the wicked forsake his way, and the unrighteous man his thoughts: and let him return unto the Lord, and he will have mercy upon him; and to our God, for he will abundantly pardon. For my thoughts are not your thoughts, neither are your ways my ways, saith the Lord. For as the heavens are higher than the earth, so are my ways higher than your ways, and my thoughts than your thoughts."

God invited the Israelites who had forsaken Him to return to Him and be restored to fellowship and blessing. They needed genuine spiritual hunger and thirst for forgiveness as a prerequisite for salvation. They needed to be restored to a right relationship with God. Like them, we must repent of our sins and draw near to God in faith. You don't have all day to take your time. You must seek God while there is still promise of his response. You should not impose your limited thoughts on God. The renewing of our hearts and minds conforms our thoughts and ways to God's. Therefore, we should not be trying to transform the church into a bunch of man-made rules and regulations contrary to God's Word.

In Isaiah 56, God includes strangers in the blessing:

"THUS, SAITH the Lord, Keep ye judgment, and do justice: for my salvation is near to come, and my righteousness to be revealed. Blessed is the man that doeth this, and the son of man that layeth hold on it; that keepeth the sabbath from polluting it, and keepeth his hand from doing evil."

Justice and righteousness co-exist they cannot be separated. So, despite what the esteemed, affluent church I attended wrongfully practiced, in God's kingdom [church/house] all people, regardless of their color, race, nationality, socioeconomic status, personal disabilities, or mental status, are all accepted with the same rights and privileges as the rest of the covenant believers. God loved and accepted each believer as one of His precious children. God's House is the house of prayer. This is where all of God's precious children should find no difference in treatment and respect. The purpose of coming together in prayer and worship is to keep each one of us in communion with God in praise, intercession, and lifting our petitions. You would think this was a no brainer but some of our purpose for going to church is twisted. We think It's about us. Our safe place to get our religious showing groove on. "Whose house?" God's house! You are merely a guest just like everyone else there to reverence God through their praise and worship. Once you fully understand God is no respecter of persons you learn how to act with genuine brotherly and sisterly love. Not with jealousy, covetousness, and envy.

Imposition of church wide fast with no genuine effort to turn from your wicked ways and follow Christ is an insult. Your lack of faith and doing your own thing contrary to God's Word wounds the entire body of believers. It shows you are not functioning on one accord and have issues with who you truly are—an identity crisis—leads to a toilet stool life!

Isaiah 58 teaches about right and wrong fasting. The people sinned so much the prophet cried out like a trumpet to God to show the house of Jacob their transgressions and sin. They were not spared. God's people hypocrisy needed to be revealed. When God's messengers do not point out the sins of His people, they are not faithful to God's call. Perhaps they rather appease man than tell him the truth. Can you believe it Judah sought God every day as if they desired to know God's ways? This was nothing more than blowing smoke in the wind a pretentious act, [like the act some of us put on] because at the same time they called on God they continued to live in sin and indifferent to His righteous Commands. It is not good to talk out of both sides of your mouth when your uttered words contradict your prayer, praise, and worship. If you have decided and admit what you are doing is a sin, and you persist in that sin because you hold the rationale that everyone sins therefore, they should not judge your sin and you find comfort in your justification: your knowledge of the truth and deliberate action to feed your flesh because it feels good, sets you apart from God.

The people of Judah served heathen gods and turned their back on God. The worship of the gods they chose involved immorality, prostitution, sorcery, and human sacrifices. Under many of these wicked leaders' Righteous believers were mistreated and perished. What gods do you hold supreme? God will let no one get away with sin. That includes you! Ask yourself why do you go to church fall on your knees, scream at the altar when you really don't want to stop sinning?

Why do you pretend in front of a congregation of people? Is it because you want to appear to delight in praising Him and act like you want to know God intimately? While at the same time you neglect God and turn your back on Him so you can pursue your earthly pleasures and gods. God is more than hospitable he sent his people an invitation and gave them an opportunity to turn from their wicked ways. You complain God doesn't help you or answer your prayers. Have you ever stopped to consider God knows your worship and fasting is hypocritical? God in Isaiah 58:3-4, made it known to them that their religious act had no value when it does not come from people who genuinely seek to obey His commandments and who are hospitable to the point, they compassionately reach out to help those in need.

> *"Wherefore have we fasted, say they, and thou seest not? Wherefore have we afflicted our soul, and thou takest no knowledge? Behold, in the day of your fast ye find pleasure, and exact all your labours. Behold, ye fast for strife, and debate, and to smite with the fist of wickedness: ye shall not fast as we do this day, to make your voice to be heard on high."*

God does not send members or visitors to your church for you to mistreat, enslave, and oppress. He approves a *fast that loosens the bands of the wicked, lifts heavy burdens, and efforts to let the oppressed go free breaking every yoke.* [Isaiah 58:6] The fast must be rooted in love for God and genuine concern for the oppressed. Just giving your tithes and offerings to the church does not free you from your responsibility to give to the poor. When you meet the needs of the poor God will approve. He will answer you when you pray. [Isaiah 58:7-12]

Is it an entirely different ballgame when you invite people to your home? The doors don't just get opened to anyone like the church doors. Your home is your sanctuary, your safe spot that would never be opened to intruders. But what about the plus one guest that comes as a friend of your invited guest? Most people will extend a warm welcome to that person unless they know something about them that provokes a cautious eye or signals a red flag. But you are the perfect host wanting nothing but to make the occasion one your guest will remember. Hebrews 13:16 *"Do not neglect to do good and to share what you have, for such sacrifices are pleasing to God"* probably rightly sums up the host intentions of wanting to throw a fabulous party. The host wants to ensure they do not neglect the guest. If they need water, it's available; Food is available, and friendly conversation, networking, and connecting with people you haven't seen for a while is a must and the key to your good party planning.

But are you open to bringing strangers into your home? Perhaps host a couple's dinner or bible study meeting at your home that may bring people you don't know? Could you do what Isaiah 58:7 says? *"Is it not to share your bread with the hungry and bring the homeless poor into your house; when you see the naked, to cover him, and not to hide yourself from your own flesh?"* [This is speaking about the fast] You might think now we are talking about something altogether different. What do you mean bring homeless people into my home? My personal space? I will not do that! It's okay though to welcome them and usher them into the church but my home. Nope!

You have a habit of neglecting the poor and least fortunate. Even if they are family members. Largely because they don't fit into your looking glass of success. There is a certain persona and atmosphere you are trying to create for your exciting evening. Less desirable family members, especially the ones who don't have proper training and lack communication skills compared to your educated and dignified guest are not invited. You don't invite them because you don't want to be embarrassed by them or spend your evening on pins and needles hoping they don't wreck your affair.

Consider the possibility of inviting people to your home to share God's message with them. Would you intentionally invite people who don't know Christ or who are on the fence about church going? Would you invite someone you don't know? Will you create a safe atmosphere for them to explore faith and encounter the love of Jesus? What are you prepared to do for Christ? Martha welcomed Jesus into her house, and she got busy hosting her guest [being a busybody?] while her sister Mary understanding the magnitude of having Jesus in her presence sat at His feet and heard His Word. She positioned herself to learn from Him. [Luke 10:38]

In Matthew 22: 1-14 Jesus taught a parable about a wedding banquet. In this parable the King sent for his invited guest. They didn't have time, so they made light of the King's invitation. The scripture says one went to his farm and another to his merchandise. The others killed the King's servants. The King sought vengeance destroyed the murders and burnt their city. The gist of this parable was that the King determined that the guest he invited [the ones who were notable, friends, and thought to be worthy] were not fit. So, he sent his servants out to gather as many people as they could find, the good and bad until they filled the wedding with guest; however, there was one person who came to the banquet unprepared. He dressed any kind of way. He was not appropriately dress for the occasion.

The King had the man bond by his hands and feet and cast into the outer darkness where weeping and gnashing of teeth awaited him. After which Jesus said: *"Many are called, but few are chosen."* [Matthew 22:14] Your takeaway from this parable is Salvation is made available to everyone but only those who respond to God's call, repent of their sins, and believe in Christ are chosen. Everyone will not wear the wedding garment because it symbolizes a condition of readiness. Will you help to make your guest ready? Are you ready?

There is a woman I know, who takes hospitality seriously. Each month, second Thursdays of every month and on other occasions, she serves with a smile. She shops for the food, snacks, beverages etc. and she hauls all the stuff into the church, meeting place. She works diligently with her team, and everyone serves with a smile. She acknowledges the visitors and takes time to bring well wishes to those celebrating birthdays. Yes, it's a thankless job but somebody has to do it and the reality is not everyone can do it like she does it. She ushers in an atmosphere of fellowship. No one truly knows what she does behind the scenes to make things happen [unless they have done it before]. We may not even know the struggles, trials, and tribulations she may have been going through to please a group of two-hundred or more women. Yet she served as others before her with a lump of mercy, a spoonful of grace, and a lot of prayer for all those who may have complained and took her unpaid service of love for granted. "Hospitality is what Hospitality does!"

This conversation began with God's warning embraced in the Visitor Parking sign. We discussed this sign in reference to Hospitality and ways we can welcome people into our church and homes to share the message of free salvation Jesus offers. But we haven't considered the flip side of the sign. What if God is saying you are a visitor in the church? Whoa! You'd say with a sigh of surprise. You may even take offense to this statement because you go to church all the time, attend bible study, attend other ministry meetings, and volunteer a lot doing church activities. So, how could you possibly be a visitor in your own church home? It's because you act like a stranger to God. You keep busy to keep score of what you have done. But do you really know Jesus? You practice worship and praise with lip service but don't get to know God for real. You don't reverence Him, and you don't keep His commandments.

How much more hospitable do people need to be to you in order for your actions to catch up with your words? Remember, God does not let sin slide. You may think you are under the radar but there will come a time where God will give you over to your reprobate mind. This means your foolish thoughts, decisions, and rationalizations that allow you to do improper things. We must be careful how we justify sin to suit our desires. If you have any sense, you will not want to experience God's wrath.

God's Word does not lie. It is not outdated, discriminatory, or divisive. The Berean Standard Bible, Roman 1:1-32 for some may be a tough pill to swallow and perhaps when they stop reading this book and discredit everything said up to this point. Trust me, discussing God's wrath against sin is God's truth the messenger must share. This is tough because we love our loved ones who decide to turn their backs against God. We pray for them without ceasing. We try not to judge them, but our hearts yearn for them. Passionate parents will love their children no matter what. They will always want to protect their babies from all things that threaten eternal life for them. Love never fails! Read the scriptures below to understand the life and death decisions our loved one's make and understand they may choose eternal life or damnation. They may turn their backs on God to satisfy their fleshly desires. It's their choice. We will love them, respect their choice, and pray for them without ceasing.

God's Wrath against Sin

**18**The wrath of God is being revealed from heaven against all the godlessness and wickedness of men who suppress the truth by their wickedness. **19**For what may be known about God is plain to them because God has made it plain to them. **20**For since the creation of the world God's invisible qualities, His eternal power and divine nature, have been clearly seen, being understood from His workmanship, so that men are without excuse. **21**For although they knew God, they neither glorified Him as God nor gave thanks to Him, but they became futile in their thinking and darkened in their foolish hearts. **22**Although they claimed to be wise, they became fools, **23**and exchanged the glory of the immortal God for images of mortal man and birds and animals and reptiles.

__24__Therefore God gave them over in the desires of their hearts to impurity for the dishonoring of their bodies with one another. __25__They exchanged the truth of God for a lie, and worshiped and served the creature rather than the Creator, who is forever worthy of praise! Amen. __26__For this reason God gave them over to dishonorable passions. Even their women exchanged natural relations for unnatural ones. __27__ Likewise, the men abandoned natural relations with women and burned with lust for one another. Men committed indecent acts with other men, and received in themselves the due penalty for their error. __28__ Furthermore, since they did not see fit to acknowledge God, He gave them up to a depraved mind, to do what ought not to be done. __29__They have become filled with every kind of wickedness, evil, greed, and depravity. They are full of envy, murder, strife, deceit, and malice. They are gossips, __30__ slanderers, God-haters, insolent, arrogant, and boastful. They invent new forms of evil; they disobey their parents. __31__They are senseless, faithless, heartless, merciless. __32__Although they know God's righteous decree that those who do such things are worthy of death, they not only continue to do these things but also approve of those who practice them.

If you know nothing else, know God will not play games with you. As Elijah said on Mt. Carmel If God is God, then follow Him. Stop being halted between two opinions. We will love you with all our hearts but hate the sin Satan has wrapped you in to snatch you from the Palm of God's hand. The good news: God invites you to turn from your wicked ways. No matter how deep you are in your sins and no matter how stuck you feel because you feel it's too late to change or turn around now, trust God. Go to God and have a genuine conversation with a pure heart and listen to his instructions or expect His wrath. My mother's prayer is to see each of my children in heaven, to hug and kiss them. God entrusted these vessels to come forth from my womb. My job is to nurture, love, and train them. God promised our children will not depart from the truth: *Train up a child in the way he should go; and when he is old, he will not depart from it.* [Proverbs 22:6] Humbly saying hope is alive because you can count on God's Word one hundred percent. Kiss your babies and love them with all of your heart, comfort them when they need and want comfort. Tissue Please! I don't want Satan to be god over any of my children or yours. They belong to God. They are God's children [even better]. God is Good! He Will deliver our children from a toilet stool life.

CHAPTER 19

Be Still And Know That I Am God

God has **Reserved** a parking space for you. We can't begin to fathom the love and mercy God has for us, but it is evident that He has a special place in His heart reserved just for His children. A reserved parking space sign is put out to indicate the spot has been reserved for a particular person, and in the spiritual realm, God has a reserved parking place for each of His children. It is a beautiful thought to visualize your reserved parking space is a permanent spot in God's heart. We are always welcome to kneel, spread out in prayer, and communicate with Him as our hearts desire. God is intentional about allowing us time and space to come into His presence; He is there when we need Him, even when we think we are moving along without Him.

What an exciting thought to know God has a permanent reserved spot for you! But how often do you actually take the time to reserve a space in your own heart specifically for God? Do you put Him first in your life, above the people, activities, and distractions that often take His place? People often try to make reservations in other areas of their lives to get prime seating, but we don't have to go through such faking or trying to impress others because God knows each of us and loves us regardless. God's love for us is so great He even reserved a parking spot in the form of His only Son, Jesus Christ. Through Jesus, we can make a reservation for eternal life if we are willing to accept Him as our Lord and Savior. He sacrificed His life for us so we could have an eternal spot in His Father's house. What a blessing it is to understand God has a prepared place for you-no one can take away. You can take comfort in knowing a permanent parking spot is reserved in the heart of our creator for each of us who choose to accept Him, and believe He loves us unconditionally. Thank God for His love and kindness!

CHAPTER 20

You Belong To God

You protect the things you own. You don't let anyone take your children or personal belongings from you without a fight. Ownership means a lot to you. When you own something, you do everything you can to protect your investment. You take care of your children, property, car, clothes, and shoes [not an extensive list]. You protect what is yours and you don't let anyone tell you what to do with your stuff: children, spouse, guns, house, money, and the list goes on.

You don't let people walk on your property and do what they want to do. "NOT HAPPENING!" Some people bear arms to deter and protect. The fact you paid your money for something makes you feel you have the right to go ballistic when someone tries to steal it. We post signs saying, "Keep Off", house protected by an alarm system or dog.

No trespassing: and many other signs to deter people. While you are doing everything to secure your fortress, children, family members and friends, you take no effort to secure and protect what belongs to God: You, "Your Soul."

Yes, you purchase life insurance to secure your beneficiaries earthly future. You get insurance to pay funeral and burial expenses. You don't want people taking up a collection to bury you. You are so focused on what happens to your remains and children when you are gone you miss out on what's going to happen to you eternally. While you were focused on leaving your beneficiaries earthly treasures, what did you do to secure the knowledge of salvation and eternal life for yourself or them? Are you a hypocrite by default? You give trinkets and things as your legacy but no training and upbringing in the Word of God where they can secure a future of eternal life. Did the stuff you left them overshadow who the real, true blessings come from? They trust you and not God. They worship you and adore you for what you have done for them and give God NADA. They won't even tithe on what you give them.

You secure and protect what's yours and have no problem killing a person who trespasses onto your property regardless of what their intent was. Question, if you can comprehend the necessity of providing for your loved ones when you die because they belong to you, why don't you protect and defend your soul which belongs to God? You have burglar alarms, high fences, motion detectors on all doors and windows, security cameras, dogs, guns, safes, and other items not listed here to warn intruders. But you don't protect your soul.

Jesus paid the price: His life for you. He died on the cross for YOUR sins. With His stripes you are healed. You belong to Him. You are His property. So, why do you take you yourself that belong to God and give yourself to another god who did not die for you and who did not create you and have no heaven or hell to put you in? Why? Why do you leave your children God graciously gave you, to Satan?

"God's Private Property, No Trespassing sign seeks to wake you up, so you can come to the realization it's a warning sign to Satan that you belong to God. Guess what? Satan already knows what you don't know. He knows he cannot trespass on God's property namely "you" unless he has permission from you or God.

> *"Beloved, we are God's children now, and what we will be, has not yet appeared; but we know that when he appears we shall be like Him, because we shall see Him as He is."* [1 John 3:2]

> *"If anyone destroys God's temple, God will destroy him. For God's temple is holy, and you are that temple."* [1 Corinthians 3:17]

> *"Not that I have already obtained this or am already perfect, but I press on to make it my own, because Christ Jesus has made me his own."* [Philippians 3:12]

God created you and loved you so much that he gave His only begotten Son, Jesus, to die on the cross for your sins so you can have eternal life. He gave you an opportunity to exercise your free will and choose to serve and honor him at no cost. Jesus paid the price! After all God has done for you, you thumb your nose up at him and run off to fornicate and prostitute yourself after Satan. You may not think you are in bed with Satan, but you are if you are obeying him and not God.

You make a choice intentionally or by omission when you fail to choose and obey God; when you fail to love Him with all of your heart; when you fail to stand up and protect your family from being devoured by Satan because you have been preoccupied with securing their earthly wealth for comfort in your death. You don't acknowledge the truth these worldly earthly possessions will perish and your property you invested in will perish. Your life insurance will perish. Your sons and daughters will perish if their souls are not secured in Jesus' name. God says, *"My sheep hear my voice, and I know them, and they follow me."* [John 10:27] When you find yourself uttering the words God do not answer my prayers, consider this, you don't hear his voice because you are not in relationship with Him. Not trying to be judgmental but our treasures are where our hearts are.

You may spend your lifetime worshipping your children and the ground they walk on, but you will not prevail if they are eternally lost and damned. *"Which is why I suffer as I do. But I am not ashamed, for I know whom I have believed, and I am convinced that he is able to guard until that day what has been entrusted to me."* [2 Timothy 1:12] God entrusted your children to you with the expectation you would give them back to him trained and equipped messengers and delivers of the Good News of Salvation through his only begotten Son, Jesus the Christ, our Lord, and Savior. Think about all the protection you put in place to ward off intruders but left yourself and children vulnerable to an eternal life of torment and gnashing of teeth at temperatures so hot you could never imagine.

Jesus loves you and willingly paid the price for your life. He did not ask you or your ancestors for one red penny for the debt He paid. He gave you eternal life at no charge with no interest rates or taxes: "Free to all who believe." And he left you with the ultimate security guard and protector, *"But the Helper, the Holy Spirit, whom the Father will send in my name, he will teach you all things and bring to your remembrance all that I have said to you."* [John 14:26]

> *"For I want you to know how great a struggle I have for you and for those at Laodicea and for all who have not seen me face to face, that their hearts may be encouraged, being knit together in love, to reach all the riches of full assurance of understanding and the knowledge of God's mystery, which is Christ, in whom are hidden all the treasures of wisdom and knowledge. I say this in order that no one may delude you with plausible arguments. For though I am absent in body, yet I am with you in spirit, rejoicing to see your good order and the firmness of your faith in Christ..."* [Colossians 2:1-23.]

You are God's Private Property you belong exclusively to Him. He is a jealous God and will not share you with imitation false gods. You should know confidently you are from God.

> *We know that we are from God, and the whole world lies in the power of the evil one. And we know that the*

Son of God has come and has given us understanding, so that we may know him who is true; and we are in him who is true, in his Son Jesus Christ. He is the true God and eternal life. [1 John 5:19-20]

"Having the eyes of your hearts enlightened, that you may know what is the hope to which he has called you, what are the riches of his glorious inheritance in the saints, [Ephesians 1:18]

SATAN IS A TRESPASSER

Satan, a trespasser, enters your property, land, life, and children without permission. He devours people who are not protected by Jesus' gift of eternal life. This includes people who are backsliders, who refuse to repent and haven't sought reconciliation and restoration. Satan is a liar, and he causes you to align with reckless thinking in avoidance of the truth. He gets you off the path of righteousness onto a path of self-destruction. You want to protect your earthly assets and give up on the eternal investment Christ made for you?

Psalms 139:13-14 reminds us of our deep connection, *"For it was you who created my inward parts; you knit me together in my mother's womb. I will praise you because I have been fearfully and wonderfully made."* God loves you and will not allow anyone to trespass or harm you without consequence. While you diligently work to monitor and protect what is yours, understand God protects what belongs to Him. If you don't belong to Him and have no intentions of belonging to Him, stop complaining about your persecuted, jacked up life. Deal with it: Your toilet stool life!

You like what Satan has to offer you, fame, fortune, riches, earned off the backs of people you have tricked and wowed with your deceitful performances and slippery tongues. You have captured the stage, and your sole performance dilutes the Word of God purposely to separate you and others from God's divine protection and order. If that is the leading role you want to play in your life, Bravo! If you want to bet fifty percent of you on God and fifty percent on Satan, you might as well hang it up. God is clear that you cannot straddle the fence and you cannot be lukewarm, God will spew you out. *16 So, because you are lukewarm—neither hot nor cold—I am about to spit you out of my mouth.* [Revelation 3:16]

> *"These are the statutes and rules that you shall be careful to do in the land that the Lord the God of your fathers, has given you to possess, all the days that you live on the earth. You shall surely destroy all the places where the nations whom you shall dispossess served their gods, on the high mountains and on the hills and under every green tree. You shall tear down their altars and dash in pieces their pillars and burn their Asherim with fire. You shall chop down the carved images of their gods and destroy their name out of that place. You shall worship the LORD your God in that way. But you shall seek the place that the LORD your God will choose out of all your*

tribes to put his name and make his habitation there.
There you shall Go… [Deuteronomy 12:1-32]

You belong to God. You know it. Yet you choose to downgrade your sinful thoughts and deeds by justifying them. You foolishly, think it is okay for you to sin because you have decided everyone sins. Why should they judge your sins. Your daddy, mother, sister, brother, friends, teachers, pastors, bosses, doctors, lawyers, confidants, colleagues, everyone sins. Your rationale is because everyone sins, no one should judge your sin. The problem with this rationale is your focus should be on God. God's judgment is what matters. God has a prepared place for you: Heaven or Hell—take your pick.

We have a habit of hanging out with people who are cool with rationalized sin. They either partake in it or falsely coach you to do what you want to do! They don't care about where you spend your eternal life. They haven't figured that out for themselves. Yet you listen to ill-advised counsel instead of God. You hang out with these unprincipled disobedient people because you feel there is no condemnation. You are willing to stake your eternal life on what they think. You want people to mind their own business and not to point out your wrong. Even if they love you unconditionally. Satan has a cure for that. He's an abuser. He wants to separate you from your family members and friends. Anyone who will tell you the truth no matter what you think.

What used to be called in the closet [really a secret life] has blossomed into man made acceptance of your sin. You were always accepted and loved as a person. You hid in the so-called closet because you knew you were sinning. You may have even known the sin itself was what your family hated. Not You! You know your mother will love you unconditionally no matter what. [Most mothers] Jesus died for you if that's not enough love, I don't know what to tell you. Have you made commitments you feel can't be undone? That's Satan's lie! God welcomes all of His children who turn from their wicked ways and repent into his protective arms of care. He loves you. Yes, your argument everyone sins is correct. We are not perfect people on our own. It took Jesus to personalize the sin He took upon himself to die for you. He covered all sins, past, present, and future. Please do not reject God's Word. Our hearts yearn to see you in heaven. Why take so much care for your life and happiness here on earth and care not about the pit of hell where you risk spending eternity? God says, *"Whoever is not with me is against me, and whoever does not gather with me scatters."* [1 John 2:15-16] *"For the time is coming when people will not endure sound teaching, but have itching ears they will accumulate for themselves teachers to suit their own passions."* [2 Timothy 4:3]

When God says do not love the world, he wants you to know the world is not your friend. It seeks to devour you. The world trespasses in your life with the intent to destroy and kill you. This world is not your home. Heed God's warning: *"Do not love the world or the things in the world. If anyone loves the world, the love of the Father is not in him. For all that is in the world—desires of the flesh and the desires of the eyes and pride of life—is not from the Father but is from the world.* [1 John 2:15-16] All this stuff, things, and possessions we were led to believe codifies our success and position was nothing but a charade! You should not be double minded and walk out your life trying to satisfy both good and evil: Talking out of both sides of your mouth.

"from the same mouth come blessing and cursing. My brothers, these things ought not to be so. Does a spring pour forth from the same opening both fresh and salt water? Can a fig tree, my brothers, bear olives, or a grapevine produce figs? Neither can a salt pond yield fresh water." [James 3:10-12] *"By this it is evident who are the children of God, and who are the children of the devil: whoever does not practice righteousness is not of God, nor is the one who does not love his brother."* [1John 3:10]

2 Timothy 3: 1-9: truthfully identifies the problem we face today:

"But mark this: There will be terrible times in the last days. ² People will be lovers of themselves, lovers of money, boastful, proud, abusive, disobedient to their parents, ungrateful, unholy, ³ without love, unforgiving, slanderous, without self-control, brutal, not lovers of the good, ⁴ treacherous, rash, conceited, lovers of pleasure rather than lovers of God— ⁵ having a form of godliness but denying its power. Have nothing to do with such people.⁶ They are the kind who worm their way into homes and gain control over gullible women, who are loaded down with sins and are swayed by all kinds of evil desires,⁷ always learning but never able to come to a knowledge of the truth. ⁸ Just as Jannes and Jambres opposed Moses, so also these teachers oppose the truth. They are men of depraved minds, who, as far as the faith is concerned, are

rejected. ⁹ But they will not get very far because, as in the
case of those men, their folly will be clear to everyone."

Protection for your soul is not to yoke yourself with unbelievers. Righteousness and lawlessness are not partners. Light does not fellowship with dark. [God separated the two] God has no accord with Satan. A believer shares no portion with an unbeliever. The temple of God has no agreement with idols. You are the temple of the living God. Says the Lord Almighty, … *"I will make my dwelling among them and walk among them, and I will be their God, and they shall be my people. Therefore, go out from their midst, and be separated from them, says the lord, and touch no unclean thing; then I will welcome you, and I will be a father to you, and you shall be sons and daughters to me."* [2 Corinthians 6:14-16]

Pray without ceasing and trust God is vigilant in monitoring and protecting your soul. He won't allow Satan to trespass and interfere with your relationship. God takes care of His children. God transformed man's Private Property No Trespassing traffic sign into God's Private Property No Trespassing sign to remind His children they belong to Him. Heed His guidance. It reduces the chance of potential conflicts and warring against yourself.

CHAPTER 21

This traffic sign is more than just an instruction to stay to the right on the road. It is a constant reminder from God you should stay right in your thinking and stay right about the things you do and speak. Staying right is being morally good, justified, and acceptable; and staying on the right side of things means there is less chance to get into trouble and do wrong. You will avoid traffic jams caused by internal conflict between your flesh and spirit.

> *"Either make the tree good and its fruit good, or make the tree bad and its fruit bad, for the tree is known by its fruit. You brood of vipers! How can you speak good when you are evil? For out of the abundance of the heart the mouth speaks. The good person out of his good treasures brings forth good, and the evil person out of his evil treasures brings forth evil. I tell you, on the day of*

judgment people will give account for every careless word they speak, for by your words you will be justified, and by your words you will be condemned." [Matthew 12:33-37]

According to Apostle Paul it is difficult to keep right all the time because there is a constant battle between the mind and the heart each pulls you in different directions towards good and evil. This traffic sign directs you to stay right and be obedient to God. There are many scriptures instructing you to keep right; from Proverbs 3:5-6: *"If you want favor with both God and man, and a reputation for good judgment and common sense, then trust the Lord completely; don't ever trust yourself. In everything you do, put God first, and he will direct you and crown your efforts with success."* to Titus 2:11-12, *"For the free gift of eternal salvation is now being offered to everyone, and along with this gift comes the realization that God wants us to turn from godless living and sinful pleasures and to live good, God-fearing lives day after day."* James 4:17," *So whoever knows the right thing to do and fails to do it, for him it is sin."* *The warning sign to keep right means to stay right not to continue in wrong living.*

You have heard the saying two wrongs don't make a right. If you stay on the path of justifying your sins by pointing out other people's sins, you choose to be disobedient and ignore God's commands. *The Lord says: These people draw near to me with their mouth and honor me with their lips, but their hearts are far from me. Their worship of me is based on merely human rules they have been taught." [Isaiah 29:13]* God is speaking about people who come before him in prayer, worship, song, and praise knowing their heart is not committed to Him or His

Word. These people govern themselves as if God's righteous standards were optional. Instead of reverencing God and His Word they resorted to filling their lives with religious rituals and traditions taught to them by their spiritual leaders and teachers who gave them a false sense of security. These same people, when the worship service is over, revert to seeking the pleasures of sin and the world to satisfy their carnal desires.

Likewise, we all know too well what it's like to associate with people who don't have genuine love for you, they use you. Fake people tell you what you want to hear, some are groupies, people who say whatever you want to stay in your presence and ride your coattail to parties, clubs, and events. While they talk about you behind your back. They manipulate you. Judging from social media traffic, people don't care if they only know two of the five-thousand people who follow them. Vanity sets in and it's all about the likes you get—the approval of man. You don't care about the posted comments that take over your Facebook page posting stuff contrary to what you believe. Some years ago, I grew tired of the liquor advertisements and other post people [I did not know] placed on what I presumed to be my social media page. [owned by Facebook not me] I went through and unfriended more than half of the followers on my page not thinking about the positive messages I could have continued to post for all to hear the Word of God.

These social media platforms are used for its owners' monetary purposes. You are given the perception you own something when you don't. They use the algorithms and other data from all participants for their purposes—you really know nothing about. To think people, have problems with big brother watching them.

To navigate through temptation and deceptive practices of this world, you must be grounded in your faith and stay "right" on the path. Don't be swayed by false promises of easy money and quick fixes. Look to God for strength and trust Him to guide you.

Approach things with diligence, avoid situations hazardous to your moral and spiritual health. This means making the right decisions, avoiding bad habits, and ultimately striving to do the right thing. Regardless of your age, background, or current circumstances, keeping right is a vital component of success and good health. But with so many temptations in your life, it's difficult to stay the course. The key to staying "right" is developing self-discipline. Choose healthy behaviors over those that lead you astray. Have the courage to turn away from things not conducive to your personal growth and well-being. Do things to promote your overall physical, mental, and spiritual health. Get an excellent support system and surround yourself with positive people who will encourage and motivate you to stay true to God's Word. This may include family, friends, spiritual advisors, counselors, and teachers. Finally, you need to rely on your faith and trust in God's help and divine intervention.

John 14:6: "*Jesus said to him, 'I am the way, and the truth, and the life.' No one comes to the Father except through me.*" "*Examine yourselves, to see whether you are in the faith. Test yourselves. Or do you not realize this about yourselves, that Jesus Christ is in you? — unless indeed you cannot meet the test!*" [2 Corinthians 13:5] "Stay Right" is an important warning sign to heed. When you see this sign posted on the roads, think of what it means from God's point of view. It will take ceaseless knee bending prayers, fasting, worshipping, and reverencing God. You are blessed. Share the good news of salvation to everyone that has ears to hear.

CHAPTER 22

No U-Turn: Don't Go Back To Your Old Ways

God gave you the ultimate gift of salvation. When you accepted this gift, you came to know Jesus, and became a New Creature, *"Therefore if any man be in Christ, he is a new creature: old things are passed away' behold all things are become new."* [2 Corinthians 5:17] You accepted Jesus Christ as your Lord and Savior for a reason. You may have been tired of living a sinful life. A life filled with drama, jealousy, empty pockets, and no job. Maybe you suffered from domestic violence and prayed as hard as you could that God would deliver you. Perhaps drugs had you captured in a life where you hurt people you never thought you would. You stole from your mama, family members, and friends. The invitation to turn your life around resonated with you and you gave your life to God. You chose not to serve Satan anymore. You felt like a monkey was lifted off your back the moment you believed.

You are expected to no longer be enslaved by the sinful things of your past. Why would you ever want to turn back to the roller coaster of hell where you almost lost your life, job, friends, or spouse? God does not want you to return to the wicked ways that preceded your salvation so, He reminds you with the No U Turn sign, so you don't make a mistake and go back to your old life.

In the Bible, there are many examples of people being warned not to go back to their old ways. In Proverbs 14:12, it says *"There is a way that seems right to a man, but in the end, it leads to death."* You cannot go against God's Word this is not the correct way. You should not try to determine what is true or false in your human wisdom because your way leads to seeds of death. God's way always leads to eternal life. When you chose Jesus, you chose eternal life.

In 1 Corinthians 6:9-10, it says,

> *"Do you not know that the wicked will not inherit the kingdom of God? Do not be deceived: Neither the sexually immoral nor idolaters nor adulterers nor male prostitutes nor homosexual offenders nor thieves nor the greedy nor drunkards nor slanderers nor swindlers will inherit the kingdom of God."*

This verse warns you if you return to these sinful practices, you will not be granted entrance into the Kingdom of Heaven. 2 Peter 2:20-22 further cautions you, saying,

"If they have escaped the corruption of the world by knowing our Lord and Savior Jesus Christ and are again entangled in it and are overcome, they are worse off at the end, than they were at the beginning. It would have been better for them not to have known the way of righteousness, than to have known it and then to turn their backs on the sacred command that was passed on to them. Of them the proverbs are true: 'A dog returns to its vomit,' and 'A sow that is washed goes back to her wallowing in the mud. "

These verses shout you must not go back to your old ways after being given the gift of salvation. *"Jesus said to him, No one who puts his hand to the plough and looks back is fit for the kingdom of God."* [Luke 9:62] Do you really want to go back to people who Trafficked you? Who tried to take your life when you escaped their abuse? Give someone another opportunity to steal your reputation and name from you? Steal Your spouse? Your Job? Think about Lot's wife. *"But Lot's wife, behind him, looked back, and she came a pillar of salt."* [Genesis 19:26] Why did she look back? Before we attempt to answer this question, it is important to know what was happening in Sodom and Gomorrah that led to Lot's wife and two daughter's exoduses.

There is nothing too hard for God. He commands His Children to keep the way of the Lord to avoid grievous sin. When you and I don't do what God commands, our sins are grievous to the extent God will take action against us. God has power and authority to accomplish what He promised. God expects parents to lead their children at home and teach them what God expects from them…the Way of the Lord. That is the Parent's responsibility to ensure their children will keep His way to do justice and judgment. God does not overlook your sin. He sees every evil, injustice, and immoral act you have committed. If you do not repent God will judge and condemn you. Sodom and Gomorrah had fallen so low they waddled in their sin and became so bold about it, they refused to repent. They were doing everything under the sun you could think of.

Lot and his family stayed in Sodom and Gomorrah during the evil and filthy deeds they witnessed. Lot tolerated the wickedness because his family gained social and material advantages. Because he allowed his family to be exposed to grievous sins, this compromise led to their tragic demise. If you do what Lot did, allow your children to be exposed to ungodly environments and evil influences for your own comfort of materialistic gain you cursed them and set them up for family tragedies.

Thanks to Abraham's prayer God saved the righteous and destroyed the guilty. In that time, the only righteous person was Lot. Lot's wife, daughters, son, and son-in laws stood to escape destruction because of their relationship with Lot. Three men, two angels and God came to Sodom. Lot greeted them with hospitality and provided nourishment to them. Before the three men could lie down, this happened:

> [4] *"Before they had gone to bed, all the men from every part of the city of Sodom—both young and old—surrounded the house.* [5] *They called to Lot, Where are the men who came to you tonight? Bring them out to us so that we can have sex with them.*

⁶ Lot went outside to meet them and shut the door behind him ⁷ and said, "No, my friends. Don't do this wicked thing. ⁸ Look, I have two daughters who have never slept with a man. Let me bring them out to you, and you can do what you like with them. But don't do anything to these men, for they have come under the protection of my roof."

⁹ "Get out of our way," they replied. "This fellow came here as a foreigner, and now he wants to play the judge! We'll treat you worse than them." They kept bringing pressure on Lot and moved forward to break down the door.

¹⁰ But the men inside reached out and pulled Lot back into the house and shut the door. ¹¹ Then they struck the men who were at the door of the house, young and old, with blindness so that they could not find the door.

¹² The two men said to Lot, "Do you have anyone else here—sons-in-law, sons or daughters, or anyone else in the city who belongs to you? Get them out of here, ¹³ because we are going to destroy this place. The outcry to the Lord against its people is so great that he has sent us to destroy it."

¹⁴ So Lot went out and spoke to his sons-in-law, who were pledged to marry his daughters. He said, "Hurry and get out of this place, because the Lord is about to destroy the city!" But his sons-in-law thought he was joking.

¹⁵ With the coming of dawn, the angels urged Lot, saying, "Hurry! Take your wife and your two daughters who are here, or you will be swept away when the city is punished."

¹⁶ When he hesitated, the men grasped his hand and the hands of his wife and of his two daughters and led them safely out of the city, for the Lord was merciful to them.¹⁷ As soon as they had brought them out, one of them said, "Flee for your lives! Don't look back, and don't stop anywhere in the plain! Flee to the mountains or you will be swept away!"

¹⁸ But Lot said to them, "No, my lords, please! ¹⁹ Your servant has found favor in your eyes, and you have shown great kindness to me in sparing my life. But I can't flee to the mountains; this disaster will overtake me, and I'll die. ²⁰ Look, here is a town near enough to run to, and it is small. Let me flee to it—it is very small, isn't it? Then my life will be spared.²¹ He said to him, Very well, I will grant this request too; I will not overthrow the town you speak of. ²² But flee there quickly, because I cannot do anything until you reach it." (That is why the town was called Zoar.)

²³ By the time Lot reached Zoar, the sun had risen over the land. ²⁴ Then the Lord rained down burning sulfur on Sodom and Gomorrah—from the Lord out of the heavens. ²⁵ Thus he overthrew those cities and the entire plain, destroying all those living in the cities—and also the vegetation in the land. ²⁶ But Lot's wife looked back, and she became a pillar of salt.

²⁷ Early the next morning Abraham got up and returned to the place where he had stood before the Lord. ²⁸ He looked down toward Sodom and Gomorrah, toward all the land of the plain, and he saw dense smoke rising from the land, like smoke from a furnace.

²⁹ So when God destroyed the cities of the plain, he remembered Abraham, and he brought Lot out of the catastrophe that overthrew the cities where Lot had lived."

[Genesis 19: 4-29]

As you can see, young and old men of the city, even the men of Sodom had looked upon the three men, the two angels and God and they wanted to have sex with them. They wanted Lot to let them get to the three men because they wanted to "Know them." [According to the Zondervan Full Life Bible, KJV commentary notes] They wanted to sexually abuse the male strangers. Zondervan shows this incident is where the word "sodomy" gained its meaning. *"It is primarily referring to homosexuality and homosexual lust. It severely condemned sodomy in the Bible (Leviticus 20:13; Deuteronomy 23:17; 1 Corinthians. 6:9; 1 Timothy. 1:8-10; and Roman 1:27)"*

It did not seem to matter to these young and old men they were trying to sexually molest God and His Angels. Their actions were grievous and immediately handled. They were smitten with blindness. Now back to the question that was asked earlier regarding why Lot's wife looked back when her life was being spared along with her daughters. Was this not enough? Some speculators say she may have wanted to retrieve some of her belongings [stuff], others say she wanted to see if the city was really going to be destroyed [unbelief]. Either way, it resulted in her death.

If you were delivered from evil and wickedness and relieved of the distress caused by the environment and circumstances, why go back to hell on earth? Can you imagine your father offering his daughters to these immoral men for their pleasures to save the men he felt responsible for because they entered his house under his hospitable protection and care? Things got worse for Lot when his daughters believing it was only them and their father left devised a plan to get him drunk to sleep with him and have children by him. Their plot worked as far as they could see, and they each had children by their father. Lot's daughters were guilty of the sin of incest. Lot's eldest daughter had a son she named Moab—Father of the Moabites and his younger daughter named her son Benammi—Father of Ammon unto this day.

The close association Lot's daughters had with the depraved people in Sodom [their father tolerated] led to their immoral depraved behaviors which resulted in his family and descendants becoming pagans. This biblical account of what happened shows you, a parent, can be faithful, righteous and keep God's commandments which may be enough to save you. But if your lifestyle is in contradiction with what you believe and you allow your children and family members to be impressionable by sinful activities, movies, friends, and environments you exposed them to, then your righteousness may not save them.

Maybe your children should not spend the night at relatives and friends' houses when you know they have some habits inconsistent with God's commandments, your lifestyle, and beliefs. And it is not your children's job to raise your children. They don't get to say how you should raise, educate, and train their siblings. No, let them raise and train their children prayerfully in the way of the Lord. They can choose to follow Lot's approach, [God forbid], and see what tragedies will befall their children. I know every grandmother and grandfather around the world will firmly shout "not on my watch…not if I can help it!"

So, No-U-Turn you must not turn back to your sinful wicked ways. God will help you before you stumble and fall. Remember, you are a New Creature, and you must strive to serve God faithfully and have confidence in Him. If you truly want to reach your destination, the No U Turn Sign can warn you, going back to your old ways is not the right way.

No one likes to feel stuck in the same spot. You want to reach your goals and live your best life. However, sometimes the journey isn't as easy as you thought. You may find yourself tempted to go back to your old ways, tempted to take the familiar route leading you to temptation and away from your goals. But the No U Turn Sign should be a reminder: going back to your old ways is not the right way. The Lord knows the way to lead you to success, and you should rely on Him to guide you there. He will never allow a temptation greater than you can handle. He will provide the strength and courage for you to resist the lure of the old paths.

When possible, avoid places that trigger you back to your old ways and seek new environments to help you further your goals. Be kind to yourself. Remember this is a journey, and you will make mistakes along the way. Don't berate yourself for trying to make a U-Turn. Instead, use it as an opportunity to learn and grow. Do not reject the Lord's guidance and stubbornly revert to your old ways, you risk derailing your progress and stagnating your growth. The Lord has given you a divine purpose and a unique life to fulfill. Embrace "**the**" path God chose for you.

CHAPTER 23

Satan's Tricks Entice You To Go The Wrong Way

Satan your adversary deceives you for one reason: to rob you of eternal life in HEAVEN!

It's important to look at how the Bible describes Satan and his deceptive ways. The Bible documents an unflattering picture of Satan, describing him as a liar and deceiver from the beginning. When Satan tempted Eve in the Garden of Eden, he used deception to manipulate her to sin against God (Genesis 3:4-5). In other parts of the Bible, he's described as a "roaring lion" that prowls around looking for someone to devour (1 Peter 5:8). Given this description, it's easy to see how Satan uses deception to influence you.

If you proclaim to be atheist, a person who don't believe in God or any gods, then Satan doesn't have to spend time sucker punching you.

He won because you have been easily deceived. You choose Satan when you deny the existence of God. *"By this it is evident who are the children of God, and who are the children of the devil: whoever does not practice righteousness is not of God, nor is the one who does not of God, nor is the one who does not love his brother."* [1 John 3:10] Satan primarily spends his time and effort going after believers. Why waste his time going after people he already has? Satan is focused on his end game: Take as many people as possible he can from God into the eternal pits of Hell with him.

I recall a time when I grew tired of AT&T's service. We switched to Comcast, and it wasn't long before I grew equally tired of them. I stuck with Comcast solely because I reasoned their customer service was a tad bit better than the other company. One thing that bothered me about both companies, is they offered excellent deals to new customers? Loyalty meant nothing to them. They didn't care that I had been a loyal paying customer for ten plus years. Only newcomers got low price offers. They locked them in for 1-2 years and then the rates would skyrocket. I wasted time and energy calling both companies customer service line only to end up disagreeing with the messenger on the phone who ultimately, said: Do you want us to discontinue your service, "mam?" They didn't care if I left. Where's the trickster in all of this? First Satan convinces you to get all these new-fangled services under the guise that you need them for convenience, status, accomplishment, or because you deserve it, and then the heart grabber: it's good for your family. Each one of your children can download apps and stream stuff to each of their devices. Of course, he hides the fact it exposes your children to many things you might not be aware of. You unlocked the key realm of Satan to them. They can pretend to be someone they are not on various social media platforms. They can talk to predators and other deceitful people you strive to keep from them. You have unlocked the pandora's box you never wanted to open. Satan gained a foothold into your home through these amenities with your permission.

So, arguing with telephone companies who provide television phone, and internet services at ridiculous prices isn't your thing. You are a gamer and like to win. You like to climb different levels and gain power packs or coins along the way. That's your thing. You play a game that teaches you to kill people and to steal from people. In one game, people steal money from other players. You are okay with the concept of taking what belongs to other people. You are okay with killing people and allowing your children to clap their hands when you have dropped a whole slew of people in the confines of the game. Satan has conditioned your mind to accept this way of thinking. So, when you see or hear something on the news about these types of things it doesn't bother you. *"In their case the god of this world has blinded the minds of the unbelievers, to keep them from seeing the light of the gospel of the glory of Christ, who is the image of God."* [2 Corinthians 4:4] *"And no wonder, for even Satan disguises himself as an angel of light."* [2 Corinthians 11:14]

More tricks of Satan and his cohorts regarding game(s) designed to steal your time and valuable resources. Some games allow you to pretend to be among the rich and famous. They built the game on you giving someone behind the scenes your hard-earned cash. Can you believe paying 6,000 dollars for a sofa in a virtual world? Buying shoes and clothing in a virtual world? Make believe fantasy hyped up to appear to be important because of what you can buy in the game. Every dollar you let go in the virtual [not real world] world is forever gone.

Perhaps Satan slapped you with a personal reality check. He told you your doctor, parents, and friends are just hating on your body. He wants you to believe your body rocks no matter how many pounds of cellulose and stretch marks you display on it. He says, Go on girl or boy strut your stuff! They are jealous of you. You can wear that crop top with your non pregnant size belly hanging out. Just get a larger size and rock it. He tricks you in to thinking your loved ones don't like you and talk about your weight to hurt your feelings. When it's a known fact that obesity kills people and causes a lot of health issues and consequences along the way. Diabetes, high blood pressure, cancer, and many health issues associated with your eating habits and lack of exercise. "Eat yourself to death," Satan laughs. He is not laughing with you; he is laughing at you. You listen to his unsolicited advice knowing he does not care about you and knowing he wants to devour you. **But you act like he's your friend.**

Satan comes into your marriage like a thief in the night. He gets you to operate in me, myself, and I manner, he knows leads to self-destruction. He has no interest in either of you raising God believing children who seek eternal life in heaven with God. Nope, he will undermine the core of your family's belief through mechanisms and toys you provide them. He knows all too well what happens to children when the parents don't have time for them because they are preoccupied with work and other things. He lurks behind parents nudging them to replace themselves with nannies and other things to keep their children taken care of and busy while they are at work. Satan does not care about your reality of having to pay bills in order to survive. He wants you to buy into that concept. He doesn't want you to strategically plan how to live on less so your children can be raised properly in the name of Jesus. Nope, that's not happening on his watch as long as he can keep you materialistic and title driven.

He destroys marriages by keeping people apart from one another. You buy into his separation plan. Where you are living separate lives under one roof, with no communication or any vibes between the two of you. Satan has a conversation with two separate people encouraging each to do what they want despite their marital vows and commitments to one another. Before you know it, Satan will have you bed hopping in infidelity and many other ungodly behaviors. I recently spoke to a friend who shared with me what I thought was a young people immoral and corrupt thing. Contracts married couples write to allow them to have a third-party partner in the martial bed. The contract is exclusive or non-exclusive. Exclusive is where the third party commits to only have sexual relations with this couple only at their beck and call and by their rules. What kind of stuff is this? Illegal yes, you'd say. Immoral definitely! Who none other than Satan pushes himself into your marital bed and entice you to commit sins of sexual immorality. His tricks entices you to live a toilet stool life so far from God. John 8:44 describes your condition,

> *"You are of your father the devil, and your will is to*
> *do your father's desires. He was a murderer from the*
> *beginning, and does not stand in the truth, because there*

is no truth in him. When he lies, he speaks out of his own
character, for he is a liar and the father of lies."

Satan tricks some women into thinking they hold their only worth
between their legs. He causes them to use what they possess to get
what they want. His slippery tongue of deceit will cause a man and a
woman to fornicate and commit adultery sins against their bodies for
temporary pleasure. Women who advanced their careers by laying on
their backs and bended knees [not in prayer] have suffered in the long
run from lack of self-esteem and confidence. Satan will lead you to a
point where you swing on poles, drinking, and using drugs because
you follow him. You have taken yourself out of God's hand and stand
at Satan's side doing his biddings. *"But I am afraid that as the serpent
deceived Eve by his cunning, they will lead astray your thoughts from
a sincere and pure devotion to Christ."* [2 Corinthians 11:3] How did
this happen?

Satan twists the truth to lead you away from God. He makes you
believe no one cares about you that you are on your own. He sows
confusion and doubt in your mind. Satan deceives you and convinces you
that what God says is not true. He knows you gain worldly satisfaction
through your sin because you want to be known by everyone in the
world. You want the center stage of your life to develop around you,
not God. You are not the first-or last-person Satan will have his way
with if you let him. He knows his limitations, yet he still goes after God
himself. For example, Satan tempted Jesus in the wilderness by trying
to get him to turn stones into bread and bow down to him (Matthew
4:1-11). Unlike you, Jesus did not do what Satan tried to tempt him

to do. *"Let no one deceive you. For that day will not come, unless the rebellion comes first, and the man of lawlessness is revealed, the son of destruction, who opposes and exalts himself against every so-called god or object of worship, so that he takes his seat in the temple of God, proclaiming himself to be God."* [2 Thessalonians 2:3-4]

Also, during the time of Job, Satan "tried to defame the character of God" by falsely accusing Job of sinning and leading him astray (Job 2:4-5). Satan enlisted his minions, men, and women to do his dirty work. *"And the great dragon was thrown down, that ancient serpent, who is called the devil and Satan, the deceiver of the entire world—he was thrown down to the earth, and his angels were thrown down with him."* [Revelation 12:9] *"Now the spirit expressly says that in later times some will depart from the faith by devoting themselves to deceitful spirits and teachings of demons."* [1Timothy 4:1]

Satan deceives you by planting false beliefs in your mind. He encourages you to doubt God's Word, question His love and plan for you, and he fills your heart with anger, fear, and despair. To counteract Satan's deceptive ways, the Bible encourages you to stand firm in your faith and put on the armor of God. See Ephesians 6:10-18 below:

> *"10 Finally, be strong in the Lord and in his mighty power.11 Put on the full armor of God, so that you can take your stand against the devil's schemes. 12 For our struggle is not against flesh and blood, but against the rulers, against the authorities, against the powers of this dark world and against the spiritual forces of evil in the heavenly realms. 13 Therefore put on the full armor of*

God, so that when the day of evil comes, you may stand your ground, and after you have done everything, to stand. [14] Stand firm then, with the belt of truth buckled around your waist, with the breastplate of righteousness in place, [15] and with your feet fitted with the readiness that comes from the gospel of peace. [16] Besides all this, take up the shield of faith, with which you can extinguish all the flaming arrows of the evil one.[17] Take the helmet of salvation and the sword of the Spirit, which is the word of God.[18] And pray in the Spirit on all occasions with all kinds of prayers and requests. With this in mind, be alert and always keep on praying for all the Lord's people."

You must remember no matter what Satan tells you, God's truth is the only truth that matters. By standing firm in your faith, you resist the lies and deception of Satan and have faith God is still on your side.

In the end, Satan is an adversary who seeks to deceive and lead you astray. But by having faith in God's truth, you can resist Satan's lies and stay firmly on the path of righteousness.

Satan seeks to lead you into making bad choices. He uses lies and deceit to manipulate you into false beliefs and false paths. But his lies and manipulation need not deceive you. With faith in God's truth, followers of Jesus, stay strong in the face of Satan's lies. By having faith in God's truth and His word, you resist the powers of darkness. God is in control and His Word will always prevail over Satan's lies. Your faith in God will keep you in Christ when Satan tries to persuade you.

Remember when facing temptation and hard decisions to take the time to pray for guidance. God will show you the path of righteousness. Trust God. Stand your ground and remain resilient in the face of Satan's schemes. How do you do this?

Through faith in God, and abiding in His love. Turn to the Bible for guidance and comfort, knowing His word never fails. Even when you fail, and are tempted to succumb to Satan's deception, you must remain confident God is faithful and ready to welcome you back with His unfailing love.

God's love is more powerful than the enemy's lies, and when you rely on Him, you overcome any challenge. The enemy may try to deceive you, but he can never change the truth of God's Word. Stay on your spiritual journey, trusting in the Lord to lead you and guide you back to Him.

No matter where you are in your journey, never forget Satan is a liar and is out to deceive. But when you stand your ground in faith, and rely on God's truth, you will remain firm and sure in the face of his schemes. God will never leave you, and His love endures forever.

Satan wants to deceive people, so they lose their way. He is mentioned in the Bible as a powerful deceiver and uses all kinds of tactics to fool people. But while Satan may be powerful, through God's Word you learn to identify and resist his deceptive devices.

The Bible says, Satan is a liar and deceiver who "has blinded the minds of those who don't believe" (2 Corinthians 4:4). He does this by distorting God's truth and presenting lies as if they were true. Scripture refers to him as "the father of lies" (John 8:44) and "the master of deception" (Ezekiel 28:15). One example of how Satan deceives people, is in the story of Adam and Eve in the Garden of Eden. Satan lied: **"You will not surely die," the serpent said to the woman. For God knows that when you eat of it your eyes will be opened, and you will be like God, knowing good and evil."** (Genesis 3:1-5). He twisted God's words to make himself look knowledgeable. Disobedience caused judgment to fall upon them:

> *"And to Adam he said, because you have listened to the voice of your wife and have eaten of the tree of which I commanded you, 'You shall not eat of it,' cursed is the ground because of you; in pain you shall eat of it all the days of your life; thorns and thistles it shall bring forth for you; and you shall eat the plants of the field. By the sweat of your face, you shall eat bread, till you return to the ground, for out of it you were taken; for you are dust, and to dust you shall return." [Genesis 3:17-19]*

Another example is the temptation of Jesus in the desert. Satan tempted Jesus with promises of power and glory if He would bow down and worship him (Matthew 4:1-11). This was a way of trying to deceive Jesus and turn him away from God. [To turn God against himself]

Satan deceives people when he leads them off the path of faith and obedience. He poses as teachers and prophets, to encourage evil and destruction (Matthew 7:15). He entices you with promises of worldly desires and distracts you from your relationship with God. No matter what form Satan's deception may take, God conquered him. Take courage in the assurance of Psalm 27:1, which says *"The Lord is my light and my salvation—whom shall, I fear? The Lord is the stronghold of my life—of whom shall I be afraid?"*

As long as you stay in God's Word and remain close to Him, He equips you to resist Satan's lies and deception. Satan aims to draw you away from God and His truth. He denies What is written in the Holy Bible and gets you to believe lies that draw you further from God. But you are not alone—with faith, you can remain standing strong against Satan's lies. The Lord is your stronghold and refuge against Satan's divisive ways, and He will never leave you no matter how hard Satan tries to pluck you from the palm of His hand.

The Lord's love for you is unending, and He will protect you from Satan's temptation and lies. God has given you His Word, a firm foundation on which you can stand. When you stand firm in your faith, trust God and His promises, you will remain secure in Him. As David said, "the Lord is the stronghold of my life—of whom shall I be afraid?" No matter how hard Satan tries to deceive and lead you astray, you must turn to God's Word for strength and courage. You must rely on the power of prayer, to ask for guidance and discernment to know what is true and what is false.

While Satan has deceived and manipulated many, God still loves you. Satan's lies are often used to distract and deceive you from knowing and living in God's truth. He may lead you astray with thoughts of doubt, fear, and worry to draw you away from God's love and Will for your life. He may also tempt you with promises of false hope and short-term gratification which can lead to long-term regret. You must not allow the lies and deception of Satan to lead you into temptation and sin, but look to the Lord for guidance and wisdom.

Here are some directives: trust God, rely on His truth, stay on the path of righteousness, don't let Satan and his minions deceive you. You need not fear Satan's plots or threats. Remain rooted in God's love and goodness, secure in the assurance He is your Father. God is more powerful than any scheme Satan can devise. Have confidence. God protects you, even when demons and wicked people work against you. Satan constantly tries to trap you and lead you away from the love of God through his cunning and manipulative tactics. While it's easy to become discouraged by Satan's weapons, know you are victorious, and can say, grave where is your sting?

The Bible has many examples of how and why Satan tries to deceive you. As just discussed, In Genesis 3, Satan tempted Eve with the promise of knowledge, and he tricked her into eating from the forbidden tree. You see how Satan deceives people by making false promises and leading them to act against God. In Matthew 4, Satan tempted Jesus in the wilderness. He told Jesus to change the rocks into bread, worship him, and throw himself off a pinnacle. In each instance, Satan tried to lead Jesus away from God's plan for him. By being aware of Satan's schemes and responding in faith, Jesus remained strong in the face of temptation.

Satan's deception also reaches beyond individual people. In Revelation 12, you find the story of the dragon, which represents Satan. He tries to deceive the world by inspiring false teaching and persecuting those who follow God. This is a powerful reminder of how Satan can work through deception to influence entire societies and cultures. Despite Satan's deceitful ways, you can stay confident in God's protection. He has given you His Word, His Spirit, and His people to help you stay true to Him and avoid Satan's schemes. With these spiritual tools, you will remain steadfast in the truth and conquer Satan. Let's say it again, Satan is an adversary who deceives. He tries to get you to turn away from God and embrace a world of sin. He tempts you with temporary gratification and sinful lifestyles, all while trying to get you to doubt God's promises. Thankfully, God has given you His Word, His Spirit, and His people to help you stay true to Him and crush Satan.

God's Word is the most powerful weapon you have. It is a window into His truth and an instruction book on how to live a godly life. The Bible reveals the deceptions of the devil, helping you recognize them before you fall prey to them. God's Word shows you how to use your spiritual armor in order to stand firm in belief. God's Spirit is your comforter, teacher, and guide. He leads you to the truth and reveals it to you through your natural spirit, prompting you to pay attention to what He is saying.

The Holy Spirit empowers you to stand against the temptation of the devil and follow Him instead. He also gives you the courage to proclaim God's truth and not get swayed by the world's smoke screens of deception. God's people are also a source of strength in the face of Satan's plots. When you come together in fellowship and unity, you fight against the lies of the devil and cling to the truth of God's Word. The support of fellow believers lifts you up when you are weak and helps you cling to God's promises amidst the onslaught of Satan's lies. God has given you all the resources you need to make sure you do not fall into Satan's traps.

You must remain vigilant, always remember Satan is the master of deception, and trust in God's Word, His Spirit, and His people to keep you safe. God's Word helps you to understand the strategies of Satan and how to resist them. You learn from God's Word what is true and what is false, and thus you can identify Satan's lies and tactics. Knowing the Word of God helps you to trust God and His promises, so your enemies do not devour you. The Holy Spirit also provides you with guidance and protection, allowing you to discern truth from lies and temptation. Once you invite the Holy Spirit to come and lead your life, He will help you stand strong in the face of temptation and deception. He will give you strength to resist the wiles of Satan.

Finally, God has given you people in the Church who can help you stay on the path of righteousness in the face of any temptation, or monkey business. You can rely on your brothers and sisters in Christ to encourage you, pray with you, and hold you accountable. Stay connected to a body of believers, so you will be held accountable and encouraged to remain in Christ. As you turn to each other for support, you rely on God's Word, His Spirit, and His people to keep you safe.

If you didn't know Satan uses people, and sometimes you, to do his dirty work this may catch you off guard. There's a thing called road rage. Without notice people can get their underwear bunched up because someone got in front of them without putting on their blinkers or they were driving too slowly. Maybe they were speeding and jetting in and out of traffic. Whatever it is, it causes some people to lose their mind. Even the calmest driver, quiet person, can be a real bear and chase people down the road because they did something wrong in their opinion. Your dandruff rises and before you know it you flipped some birds and screeched your tires out of anger.

Maybe you want a job you know your coworker is best suited for but you want it so you sabotage the person's work, and reputation so you could get the job. Some people are good at stealing opportunities from people and stabbing them in their backs. Satan entices well-known actors and actresses you grew to respect to lure you into sinful acts and deeds.

DON'T DO THINGS THE WRONG WAY

We will discuss what happens when you do things the wrong way. God warns you against worldliness and boasting about tomorrow. James 4:1-17 sets the tone for what happens when you do things the wrong way:

> "**4** *What causes quarrels and what causes fights among you? Is it not this, that your passions are at war within you?* ² *You desire and do not have, so you murder. You covet and cannot obtain, so you fight and quarrel. You do not have, because you do not ask.* ³ *You ask and do not receive, because you ask wrongly, to spend it on your passions.* ⁴ *You adulterous people! Do you not know that friendship with the world is enmity with God? Therefore, whoever wishes to be a friend of the world makes himself an enemy of God.* ⁵ *Or do you suppose it is to no purpose that the Scripture says, "He yearns jealously over the spirit that he has made to dwell in us"?* ⁶ *But he gives more grace. Therefore, it says, "God opposes the proud but gives grace to the humble."* ⁷ *Submit yourselves therefore to God. Resist*

the devil, and he will flee from you. ⁸ Draw near to God, and he will draw near to you. Cleanse your hands, you sinners, and purify your hearts, you double-minded. ⁹ Be wretched and mourn and weep. Let your laughter be turned to mourning and your joy to gloom. ¹⁰ Humble yourselves before the Lord, and he will exalt you.¹¹ Do not speak evil against one another, brothers The one who speaks against a brother or judges his brother, speaks evil against the law and judges the law. But if you judge the law, you are not a doer of the law but a judge.¹² There is only one lawgiver and judge, he who is able to save and to destroy. But who are you to judge your neighbor?¹³ Come now, you who say, "Today or tomorrow we will go into such and such a town and spend a year there and trade and make a profit"—¹⁴ yet you do not know what tomorrow will bring. What is your life? For you are a mist that appears for a little time and then vanishes. ¹⁵ Instead you ought to say, "If the Lord wills, we will live and do this or that." ¹⁶ As it is, you boast in your arrogance. All such boasting is evil. ¹⁷ So whoever knows the right thing to do and fails to do it, for him it is sin."

Think about verse one. What causes you to quarrel and fight? It doesn't seem to take much these days for a fight to ensue. People quarrel about money. Tensions rise when people refuse to payback money they borrowed. Relationships tarnish because of disputes over money. It's not always quarrels that erupt because someone didn't pay you your money, but we know street fights occur around criminal activities involving money. I will never forget how friends and family members quarrel about numbers they played back in the day and the number man's failure to pay up! People had rent parties. They gambled with their family members and friends and won their money playing card games. Today money often stimulates quarrels and fights, but it's also centered on relationships. Cat fights over boyfriend stealing. "You took my man" nonsense. Seems nonsense, but it resulted in the death of a teenage girl who was an honor student. I recently heard a story where a mother, jealous of a woman who was seeing her boyfriend, sent her teenage daughters to take care of the matter. The fiasco resulted in the death of both her daughters.

Do you get to where your passions war inside of you causing you to react to situations the wrong way? The scripture says that you covet what you cannot have so you quarrel and fight. Jealousy is more than a notion. It's real. You do strange things. [acting out of character] You want what other people have. You have worked years to get the few things you have gained. But you see other people gaining titles and positions because of who they know. Not because they were skilled or hardworking. God said you asked and did not receive because you asked wrongly for things to spend it on your passions. You cannot win by doing things the wrong way. *"Whoever knows the right thing to do and fails to do it, for him it is sin."* [James 4:17]

"No temptation has overtaken you that is not common to man. God is faithful, and he will not let you be tempted beyond your ability, but with the temptation he will also provide the way of escape, that you may endure it." [1Corinthians 10:13] You are not the first person to be tempted

by Satan to do his biddings. The quarrels and fights are his methods to cause dissension. It's his way to stirrup your old ways to make you put your "religion" aside in that moment, doing things contrary to God's Will. The wrong way sign points to John 3:19-21 where you get a glimpse of your status with God:

"And this is the judgment: the light has come into the world, and people loved the darkness rather than the light because their works were evil. For everyone who does wicked things hates the light and does not come to the light, lest his works should be exposed. But whoever does what is true comes to the light, so that it may be clearly seen that his works have been carried out in God."

Are your works evil? Do you bear false witness against your neighbor, colleague, or friend because you don't like them? Because they have what you don't have? Are you the person who does what is true and what is right—You do things the right way? You can't be a friend of the world and God's friend too. It doesn't work that way. God opposes the proud and gives grace to the humble. You should do everything you do in word and deed in the name of the Lord Jesus, and you should give thanks to your Father, God. [Colossians 3:17] God does not want you to grow weary of doing good. God promises you will reap in due season. [Galatians 6:9] It is so hard to wrap your heart around God's timing. Sometimes it feels like it took God a million years to move the mountain in your life so you could escape the avalanche behind it. Yes, you work hard for your money, and you don't want anyone telling you what to do with it. You spend it the way you want too but you run back to God for replenishment having sown nothing in the kingdom of God. You walked passed the poor and argued with signs people held up saying they will work for food.

You don't have to respond to mean people with an old-fashioned tongue lashing. Quiet as it is kept that won't work anyway today. Be careful about who you speak to these days because folk will show up on your doorstep. *"Do not be overcome by evil, but overcome evil with good."* [Romans 12:21] When you turn the other cheek, "Say What?" you put an end to quarrels and fights. You can turn the page to new beginnings and new opportunities. Misunderstandings don't have to escalate to loss of life and reputation. Do the opposite of the wrong thing, do the right thing. This sign is God's reminder you belong to him. *"Let your light shine before others, so that they may see your good works and give glory to your Father who is in heaven."* [Matthew 5:16] A couple paragraphs ago, you were asked what causes you to quarrel or fight? Did you come up with an answer? Take a moment to reflect on your answer and consider what you would do differently given the chance.

The "Wrong Way" to handle things is when you convince yourself you need to take matters into your own hands. When you refuse to ask God what you should do the outcome might take your freedom away. Grade school kids' response to conflict is easily understood to be childish. They may push and shove each other around or cross their arms saying, "I am not your friend anymore." Once they express their feelings it's over. Done, Done, and Done. Teenagers take things to a different level. They don't like people looking at them and a fight can erupt just for looking at someone. Being two faced doesn't help either. Social media can be an incubator for socialites waiting to explode when people don't like their post and their friends have more followers than they do. It's sad when a young person takes his or her own life because of social media bullies. Adults should know better. Whatever issues you have with someone, go to them directly and seek peace. Of course, ask God first and ask God to prepare the heart of the person you need to speak with. *"If any of you lacks wisdom, let him ask God, who gives generously to all without reproach, and It will be given to him."* [James 1:5] also *"Beloved, never avenge yourselves, but leave it to the wrath of God, for it is written, 'Vengeance is mine, I will repay, says, the Lord."* [Romans 12:19]

If you want to avoid a traffic jam and the drama in your life, do not overlook the "Wrong Way" traffic sign. The Bible has many examples of people going the wrong way and doing the wrong things and the consequences they faced because of it. We see in judges what people do when there are no authority figures or leaders around. In Judges 17:6 and 21:25 the scripture says, *"In those days there was no King in Israel, and every man did that which was right in his own eyes."* You know where this conversation is going. People who do right in their own eyes eventually do what is evil in the eyes of God. People want to do their own thing that includes sleeping around with multiple people, hanging out with the wrong crowd, doing things behind people's back, taking things that don't belong to them and the list goes on. You can bet in the Kings presence people gave him pleasantries and obeyed his commands. But when he was gone, not available, out of town, they ignored him and had a funky good time in his absence. You ignore God in the same way. Just because you don't see Him, or you think you are hidden from Him; you act like a fatherless child.

If you disobey God, be prepared to suffer the consequences. Most times when you start wrong, you end wrong. Advertisers (enticers) make a living by getting you to buy what they are selling. In today's society sex, drugs, and alcohol are the key ingredients to what some would term a good time. Even Apostle Paul acknowledged that doing the right thing is hard. He said, *"I find then a law, that, when I would do good, evil is present with me."* [Romans 7:21] According to Apostle Paul, you don't have to go far to find trouble.

When parents leave home, teenagers might throw a party in their absence and serve the essential good time ingredients to those in attendance. No authority figure at the house [the crib, your spot] is an opportunity for mishap. You have good intentions to do the right thing; But you struggle with doing what you know is right. You are not your own master. Evil and sin rules you if you are not in Christ. Christ will make a way for you to escape temptation if you are His. The Apostle Paul understands warfare is continual against those who limit the work of God in their life. Sin will fight to keep control over you. Your flesh sins against you. You may wrestle with your flesh day and night. You must constantly decide whether you will surrender to your sinful nature or to God's divine nature. You only have one life to get this right. You must put to death your sinful ways otherwise you are spiritually dead. The Spirit leads you when you put to death regularly the sinful deeds of your body. *Whoever has my commandments and keeps them, he is who loves me. And he who loves me will be loved by my Father, and I will love him and manifest myself to him."* [John 14:21]

"No servant can serve two masters, for either he will hate the one and love the other, or he will be devoted to the one and despise the other. You

cannot serve God and money." [Luke 16:13] *"Not everyone who says to me, 'Lord, will enter the kingdom of heaven, but the one who does the will of my Father who is in heaven. On that day many will say to me Lord, Lord, did we not prophesy in your name, and cast out demons in your name, and do many mighty works in your name? And then will I declare to them, I never knew you; depart from me, you workers of lawlessness."* [Matthew 7:21] So, going the wrong way and doing things the wrong way gets you a double whammy: Stopped traffic jam on the freeway of your life on a hot sunny day in Atlanta on highway 400 not moving more than an inch every thirty minutes.

Okay, you get it. Don't disobey God's Wrong way warning sign and don't do the wrong thing. So, how do you do the right thing? By living right! And how do you live right?

> *"Now there was a man of the Pharisees named Nicodemus, a ruler of the Jews. This man came to Jesus by night and said to him, Rabbi we know that you are a teacher come from God, for no one can do these signs that you do unless God is with him. Jesus answered him, 'Truly, truly, I say to you, unless one is born again, he cannot see the kingdom of God.' Nicodemus said to him, How can a man be born when he is old? Can he enter a second time into his mother's womb and be born? 'Jesus answered, 'Truly, Truly, unless one is born of water and the Spirit, he cannot enter the kingdom of God..." [John 3:1-36]*

There's your answer nestled in John 3:1-16. You must be born again. Read on!

CHAPTER 24

There Is No Other Way!

There is only one way to eternal life in heaven. It's through Jesus, the Christ, our Lord, and Savior. **THERE IS NO OTHER WAY**! Your mother, father, god parents, sisters, brothers, boyfriend, girlfriend, colleagues, sorority sisters, fraternity [Frat Bros] or friends do not have "the hook up card" to help you by-pass hell to heaven. It's not the Monopoly "get out of Jail free pass." If the hook up doesn't include the path to salvation through Jesus, it's nothing. The most important decision you will ever make in life is the choice of whether you will obey the one-way signs pointing you toward salvation. Whether it is the physical signs of traffic control, or the spiritual warnings of the Bible, you must make the choice to obey and follow the warning or face the consequences. Many have experienced the dangers of not following the physical one-way traffic signs, often leading to an accident or a ticket. However, the spiritual one-way sign, is even more important, because it leads to eternal salvation or condemnation.

According to the Bible, the only one way to be saved is through Jesus Christ.

In John 3:1-21 Jesus teaches Nicodemus about what he must do to be saved:

> "**Now** *there was a Pharisee, a man named Nicodemus who was a member of the Jewish ruling council.* [2] *He came to Jesus at night and said, "Rabbi, we know that you are a teacher who has come from God. For no one could perform the signs you are doing if God were not with him."* [3] *Jesus replied, "Very truly I tell you, no one can see the kingdom of God unless they are born again."* [4] "How can someone be born when they are old?" Nicodemus asked. "Surely they cannot enter a second time into their mother's womb to be born!"*
>
> [5] *Jesus answered, "Very truly I tell you, no one can enter the kingdom of God unless they are born of water and the Spirit.* [6] *Flesh gives birth to flesh, but the Spirit gives birth to spirit.* [7] *You should not be surprised at my saying, 'You must be born again.'* [8] *The wind blows wherever it pleases. You hear its sound, but you cannot tell where it comes from or where it is going. So, it is with everyone born of the Spirit."* [9] "How can this be?" Nicodemus asked.* [10] *"You are Israel's teacher," said Jesus,*

"and do you not understand these things? [11] Very truly I tell you, we speak of what we know, and we testify to what we have seen, but still, you people do not accept our testimony. [12] I have spoken to you of earthly things and you do not believe; how then will you believe if I speak of heavenly things?[13] No one has ever gone into heaven except the one who came from heaven—the Son of Man [14] Just as Moses lifted up the snake in the wilderness, so the Son of Man must be lifted up, [15] that everyone who believes may have eternal life in him."

[16] For God so loved the world that he gave his one and only Son, that whoever believes in him shall not perish but have eternal life. [17] For God did not send his Son into the world to condemn the world, but to save the world through him. [18] Whoever believes in him is not condemned, but whoever does not believe stands condemned already because they have not believed in the name of God's one and only Son. [19] This is the verdict: Light has come into the world, but people loved darkness instead of light because their deeds were evil.[20] Everyone who does evil hates the light, and will not come into the light for fear that their deeds will be exposed. [21] But whoever lives by the truth comes into the light, so that it may be seen plainly that what they have done has been done in the sight of God."

Nicodemus came to speak with Jesus privately and started the conversation with information Jesus already knew. One might surmise

Nicodemus was really trying to test Jesus. After all, we presume Nicodemus is not a goof ball since he was a Pharisee who was a member of the ruling council. As you can see Jesus told Nicodemus he must be born again. I can only speculate what went on in Nicodemus brain when he tried to process how he could get back in his mother's womb to get born again. Now I know this may sound ridiculous if you have never heard this scripture before. The point of sharing this is to let you know you must believe Jesus is the Son of God as stated in verse 16. Your belief in Jesus guarantees you will not perish but have eternal life. [John 3:16] This scripture confirms the only way to heaven is through Jesus the Christ.

There may be people who believe there are other ways to get saved. Do everything you can to help them understand there is only one way. Jesus is the only way to gain eternal life and salvation from God's eternal wrath. Through Jesus you receive the gift of atonement and forgiveness for your sins. You can follow Jesus's way and receive His blessings through His grace. It is up to you to make the choice to either follow the physical one-way signs and obey the laws of man only, or follow the spiritual one-way sign and obey God. Choosing the wrong path can have devastating consequences, but God gives you a way of escape and it is through Jesus. The same God who created you with the expectation you will be with him in heaven, also provides you with the Holy Spirit as a comforter and advocate. He equips you with spiritual gifts and gives you the strength and courage to accept and follow the one-way sign toward eternal life.

No matter your station in life, you can receive God's anointing and forgiveness. God does not require you to be brilliant, wealthy, famous or titled. He wants you to obey Him and to accept His guidance, no matter how hard it seems at times. In the end, following the one-way sign [Jesus Christ] will bring you abundant life and eternal peace. God knows the path to true joy and fulfillment is through living according to His will. Living according to God's will requires you to listen to His Word, to be aware of His direction and intent, and to obey His commands regardless of the cost or difficulty. This isn't always easy, especially when our culture does not always value spiritual living or prioritizing God's Will over our own.

In these moments, it is essential to remember God's promise of an eternal reward. Following His one-way sign brings a peace that surpasses all understanding, no matter the cost. God cares deeply for you, unconditionally loving you despite your faults and failures. He provides you with a clear path to abundant life if you follow it. Whether it means taking a detour away from a dead-end street or turning back toward a place of safety, God's one-way sign always points you toward genuine joy and fulfillment. To put it simply, He desires you to be obedient to His plan, so you can experience the eternal peace and abundant life He has promised you.

You don't have to worry about distractions and temptations because you know God will lead you in the right direction. With His help, you will rise above the challenges and live a life of purpose and contentment. God will protect you and keep you safe as you journey down the one-way path toward eternal life.

CHAPTER 25

We define a detour as *a long roundabout that is taken to avoid something or to visit somewhere along the way and an alternative route for use by traffic when the usual road is temporarily closed.* The detour provides opportunities for you to avoid traffic jams in your life. The detour ahead sign is the metaphorical representation of unanticipated obstacles you face in life. I am guessing you have encountered a few detours where the unexpected obstacles halted your footsteps to the extent you didn't know what to do. Although detours seem inconvenient, they can actually be a blessing in disguise.

God uses the detours to help you grow, learn, and to prepare you for the next stages of your life. This is where you need to use the caution sign and seek God on how to proceed because Satan throws a few monkey wrenches on your path, detours designed to distract you and lead you on a path away from God, a round-about you can't seem to exit. You definitely don't want to avoid God and chase your tail at the same time.

Take Moses for example, he endured a forty-year detour in the wilderness before being called by God to lead his people out of bondage. During this time, God taught Moses the leadership qualities he needed in order to lead his people out of slavery. If you know Moses' story, your response might be: "What! That's not how I recall the story." You like most of us probably don't focus on God's role in Moses' growth and development. Instead, you focused on the ungrateful, disrespectful, complaining troublemakers, people who always cry foul. Forty seems to be the number for Moses. Moses was 40 years old when he avenged an Israelite by murdering his oppressor. He exiled himself to Midian and spent 40 years there where he took his first wife, and it was after 40 years had passed when an angel appeared to Moses in the flames of a burning bush in the desert near Mount Sinai. [Acts 7:30; Acts 7:23-24…30] He had been in the Desert 40 years.

You know from the scripture Moses and his brother Aaron obeyed God's voice and went to Pharaoh and demanded he let God's people go. God sent ten plagues on Egypt before Pharaoh caved in. The people complained about the possibility of being swept away in the waters of the Red Sea. They doubted Moses' authority and of course his leadership abilities. How many times have you found yourself in Moses' shoes? Perhaps your employees have no skin in the game except working for their paychecks think they know more than you and tell you how to run your business. Maybe it's your parishioners who have a lot to say about what you should preach and teach at your church since they think they have a better connection to God than you.

Perhaps your children think they are the parents, and they don't give you credit for being the responsible adult who has their best interest at heart. They only listen to you when they want something or when something is in it for them. Maybe people frown upon you because of your untitled status. They look down on you because you don't have what they have. You don't have money, a house, fancy car, or fancy clothes. God called Moses to deliver the Israelites from Pharoah's oppressive grip but there may have been people among them who did not want to leave the oppressive but stable life they learned to cope with. They had a place to sleep and food.

While many of their comrades cried to God for deliverance, some did not. Like Lot's wife and daughters, some people were saved because of their relationship with the righteous. When you think about what Harriet Tubman, born Araminta Ross, A.K.A. Moses, had to do to protect those who believed in her God given ability to lead them from the shackles of slavery both the skeptical and afraid you can only imagine the criticism she endured from those she helped but she pressed on.

Moses had to press on too. Despite the complaints of the Israelites. Hear their grumblings in the scriptures below in Exodus 14:1-18: below

> *"¹⁰ When the Israelites saw the king coming with his army, they were frightened and begged the Lord for help. ¹¹ They also complained to Moses, "Wasn't there enough room in Egypt to bury us? Is that why you brought us out here to die in the desert? Why did you bring us out of Egypt anyway? ¹² While we were there, didn't we tell you to leave us alone? We'd rather be slaves in Egypt than die in this desert!"¹³ But Moses answered, "Don't be afraid! Be brave, and you will see the Lord save you today. These*

*Egyptians will never bother you again. [14] The Lord will fight for you, and you won't have to do a thing."[15] **The Lord said to Moses**, "Why do you keep calling out to me for help? Tell the Israelites to move forward. [16] Then hold your walking stick over the sea. The water will open up and make a road where they can walk through on dry ground. [17] I will make the Egyptians so stubborn that they will go after you. Then I will be praised because of what happens to the king and his chariots and cavalry. [18] The Egyptians will know for sure that I am the Lord."*

Once the Israelites reached the other side of the Red Sea, after witnessing God parting the sea for their safe passage and seeing "with their own eyes" what God did to the king, his chariots and cavalry, and after seeing the bodies of the men and their horses drown, they worshiped and trusted God and his servant Moses. In Exodus 15: 1-18 Moses and the Israelites sang this song in praise of the Lord:

"I sing praises to the Lord for his glorious victory! He has thrown the horses and their riders into the Red sea.[2] The Lord is my strength, the reason for my song, because he has saved me. I praise and honor the Lord—he is my God and the God of my ancestors.[3] The Lord is his name, and he is a warrior![4] He threw the chariots and army of Egypt's king into the Red Sea, and he drowned the best of the king's officers.[5] They sank to the bottom just like stones.[6] With the tremendous force of your right arm, our Lord, you crushed your enemies.[7] What a

great victory was yours, when you defeated everyone who opposed you. Your fiery anger wiped them out, as though they were straw. [8] *You were so furious that the sea piled up like a wall, and the ocean depths curdled like cheese.* [9] *Your enemies boasted that they would pursue and capture us, divide up our possessions, treat us as they wished, then take out their swords and kill us right there.* [10] *But when you got furious, they sank like lead, swallowed by ocean waves* [11] *Our Lord, no other gods compare with you— Majestic and holy! Fearsome and glorious! Miracle worker!* [12] *When you signaled with your right hand, your enemies were swallowed deep into the earth.*

[13] *The people you rescued were led by your powerful love to your holy place.* [14] *Nations learned of this, and trembled Philistines shook with horror.* [15] *The leaders of Edom and of Moab were terrified. Everyone in Canaan fainted,* [16] *struck down by fear. Our Lord, your powerful arm kept them still as a rock until the people you rescued to be your very own had marched by.*

[17] *You will let your people settle on your own mountain, where you chose to live and to be worshiped.* [18] *Our Lord, you will rule forever!"*

Exodus 14:20-21

"²⁰ *Miriam the sister of Aaron was a prophet. So, she took her tambourine and led the other women out to play their tambourines and to dance.* ²¹ *Then she sang to them:*

"Sing praises to the Lord
for his great victory!
He has thrown the horses
and their riders into the sea."

They were truly excited God had delivered them from their enemies. Those people who despitefully used and abused them. They were grateful to be safe and alive in the moment. It wasn't long after the singing and rejoicing they complained about being thirsty. [Exodus 14:25-27] Then on the fifteenth day of the second month after they escaped from Egypt they complained to Moses and Aaron about hunger. Here is what they said and God's response to their complaints:

² *There in the desert they started complaining to Moses and Aaron,* ³ *"We wish the Lord had killed us in Egypt. When we lived there, we could at least sit down and eat all the bread and meat we wanted. But you have brought us out here into this desert, where we are going to starve."*

⁴ *The Lord said to Moses, "I will send bread down from heaven like rain. Tell the people to go out each day and gather only enough for that day. That's how I will see if they obey me.* ⁵ *But on the sixth day of each week they must gather and cook twice as much."*

These verses are shared with you to help you understand if you don't already, people will sing you praises, respect you, and even follow you if they get what they want. This "ride and die stuff" is not authentic. When I began practicing criminal law shortly after being licensed to practice, I encountered men with known reputations on the street of being the beast. They weren't snitches. I often heard the phrase "snitches get stitches." I believed this at the beginning of my career until I quickly learned snitches who cooperated earlier in the game reduced their chances of receiving long-term prison sentences. I also learned most times; the state and federal prosecutors already knew most of the players in the scenario and information beyond what my clients knew. Why? Because their "boys" snitched on them. The government followed what I called the food chain plucking the fruit from the bottom until they got to the top.

The Bible tells us about Simon Peter who swore he would never deny Christ or turn his back on him. Shortly after Jesus was taken into custody. In John 18:15-27 we see Peter when asked on three different occasions if he was a disciple of Christ, in front of accusers who saw him with Christ. Peter denied the allegations, and the rooster crowed. In today's language the questions may have been posed differently like: isn't Christ your home boy? Your Homie? Weren't you running with Christ? I think I saw you cut this dude's ear off when you were with him.

If my client had not copped a case, perhaps his so-called friend informants would have hidden in fear and kept their mouths shut as long as the police could not find them. Getting back to Moses. Food fell from heaven to feed the complainers who acted like they were going to starve to death after God saved them. Yeah, I know "Ye of little faith."

The Israelites stood on a great promise God made to Abraham before he died. God promised to give his people a Promised Land, flowing with milk and honey. When they reached the outskirts of the Promised Land, spies were to survey the land they were to possess. Ten of the spies gave bad reports about the land. They reported the people there were stronger than them so they could not attack. Their lack of belief and grumblings caused God to discipline them. None of their generation was allowed to step into the land. That is why they wandered in the desert wilderness for 40 years. Moses died and went to be with God at Mt. Nebo, just outside the Promised Land. Below is God's response to their continued complaints which led to God's disciplinary action:

> *"The Lord said to Moses and Aaron: How long will this wicked community grumble against me? I have heard the complaints of these grumbling Israelites. So, tell them, 'As surely as I live, declares the Lord, I will do to you the very thing I heard you say: In this wilderness your bodies will fall—every one of you twenty years old or more who was counted in the census and who has grumbled against me. Not one of you will enter the land I swore with uplifted hand to make your home, except Caleb, son of Jephunneh and Joshua, son of Nun."* [Numbers 14:27-30]

As you can see, the detours suffered by the Israelites were caused because of their lack of faith, disbelief, and selfishness. Their constant groanings, grumblings, and complaints caused the generation to suffer and die in the wilderness of the life their lack of faith and disbelief created for them. Be careful what you say. Their tongues sentenced them to death.

How many times has God delivered you from something in your life? How long after your deliverance did you lift your hands up, worshiped, praised, and thanked him for bringing you out of the mess you were in? How long after your deliverance, [winning your court case, getting vindicated, having your reputation restored, gaining your freedom from your oppressors, those who held you as property, sold you for sex, and abused you] did it take for you to complain to God about something else as if He has done nothing for you? Are your children cursed because of your tongue? Because of words you have spoken over them? Because of something you did to advance their education and or careers knowing what you were doing was wrong and creating an unfair advantage for them? Were your mishaps or misgivings one of Satan's designed detours to steer you the wrong way? Or was it a lesson from God to teach you something?

There are others who experienced detours on their journey. The Apostle Paul also experienced a year detour in the desert, where God removed the cultural life in order to strengthen him, teach him, and develop his calling. One of the most significant examples is found in the life of Abraham. Abraham was obedient to God even when he was asked to travel to a foreign land. We can see how God directed and changed the course of his life many times. Abraham was called out from all he knew, to pursue the will of God. He was told to leave his home and his people and to go to a place He would get from God. But when Abraham arrived there, he faced difficulties, from famine to warfare. Yet God was faithful to direct him, protect him, and bless him.

Isaiah spoke of true obedience being rewarded with rewards. He said, *"Obedience is better than sacrifice, and to hearken than the fat of rams."* [Isaiah 1:19] The Bible refers to detours often and Christians should take heed to these warnings from God in order to avoid the pitfalls of a spiritual detour. You can avoid detours by following the guidance of the Holy Spirit and heeding warnings from God. Detours can be a sign of God's will in your life, and these struggles can actually help you to grow and learn. The point of your life is to reach your ultimate destination, eternity in Heaven. Detours can be an important part of the process as they can help you get back on the right path and provide you with the wisdom and strength, you need to reach your goal. You can learn from your detours and stay on the right path by allowing God to direct your path.

One of the greatest truths of Christianity is that no matter what obstacles, trials, and detours that you face, God is sovereign and in control. He knows what lies ahead and He will direct you in the way you should go. You may face unexpected difficulties and challenges, but with faith, trust, and prayer, you will be able to overcome them.

The Bible has many examples of people facing detours in their lives. Another example of detours in the lives of God's people is found in the life of Joseph. He was sold into slavery and eventually made it to a place of honor in Pharaoh's court. But he was betrayed by his brothers and falsely accused by Potiphar's wife. Despite all this, God was with him, and He used these detours to eventually position Joseph to save God's people from starvation.

We also see Jesus Himself faced detours in His life. He had a mission to fulfill, but He often faced opposition. He dealt with people who didn't understand His teachings, and He faced the ultimate challenge of His death on the cross. Even this detour was part of God's plan, to bring redemption and salvation to all. As a Christian, you can rely on God to keep you on course, even when you face detours and setbacks. He will use your difficulties to shape you and help you to grow in faith. You can look to the examples of the Bible to see how God directed his people and gave them hope and courage to face whatever lied ahead. As you trust in Him, He will bring good out of your detours and transform your life for His purpose and glory.

CHAPTER 26

LOVE YOUR NEIGHBORS
"For Real"

How Can We Love One Another Despite Our Differences?

We are talking about this right here and now because the world is strange to us and is indifferent regarding the Word of God. People are suffering and innocent children are dying for senseless reasons. Angry People are killing people. Maybe their anger is triggered because someone bullied them in the past. Some people grew up without parents. They had to find love and survive the foster care system. Some lack self-esteem. Some people stole from them and sexually abused them; Someone took their love partner; or they lost their job. Some of these things can cause people to suffer socially and mentally.

The worst things become, the more people get numb from it all and slip into Judgment or I don't care Zones. There are people who have hated a group of people for so long because of their religious beliefs, skin color, ethnic group, socioeconomic status, and education that they really don't know why they are carrying the hatred of their parents or ancestors in this day and age. They may not even remember why they hate certain people anymore.

You might find it hard to show love to others, especially when they have different opinions, values, and beliefs than you. However, this doesn't mean you are unable to find common ground and learn to love each other despite your differences. You don't have to pick up a gun and go out and shoot innocent people. Most of the time people are killing people who had nothing to do with what happened to them. One of the best ways to start understanding and loving each other is by delving into our common ancestry. According to Genesis 1-9, all of our ancestors were united as one united people in a single language until they attempted to build a tower that reached the heavens, [they had ill intent] God confused their language, so they were unable to understand each other. From there, the Lord scattered them around the world.

Although our language, cultures, and beliefs have changed greatly since then, we are still connected by our common ancestor, Adam, and his wife, Eve. It is perplexing to comprehend why there are people who roam this world with the inability to understand that each and every person walking on this planet are descendants of Adam and Eve. We are their children, their descendants. We know the story of Cain and Abel. That story doesn't help with showing us how to love one another unconditionally but it's an illustration of how two men, brothers, Cain, and Abel raised by the same parents were different to the point that

Cain took his brother's life and committed the first murder that is forever recorded and talked about.

God spends an incredible amount of time allowing his children to exercise "free will." God allows us to decide whether we will accept Jesus the Christ, His only begotten Son, as our Lord and Savior. But before we get to the Crucifixion of a sinless man, Jesus, [see the emergency exit section for more on this] the Bible unfolds many times when man chose different views, opinions, values, and beliefs that disagreed with God.

One example is the calling out of our ancestors on Mt. Carmel. Elijah challenged them concerning their idol gods, he asked them how long they were going to be halted between two opinions. This is a prime example of children in the same family exercising their "Free Will" in a different way even if it's contrary to the Will of God who created them. They chose to follow idols and worship other gods despite God's warnings. The bible's account of what happened on Mt. Carmel demonstrates the death wages of sin.

Let's take a look at 1 Kings 18:20-40:

> *²⁰ So Ahab sent for all the children of Israel, and gathered the prophets together on Mount Carmel. ²¹ And Elijah came to all the people, and said, "How long will you falter between two opinions? If the Lord is God, follow Him; but if Baal, follow him." But the people answered him not a word. ²² Then Elijah said to the people, "I alone am left a prophet of the Lord; but Baal's prophets are four hundred and fifty men. ²³ Therefore let them give us two bulls; and let them choose one bull for themselves, cut it*

in pieces, and lay it on the wood, but put no fire under it; and I will prepare the other bull, and lay it on the wood, but put no fire under it. ²⁴ Then you call on the name of your gods, and I will call on the name of the Lord; and the God who answers by fire, He is God."

So, all the people answered and said, "It is well spoken."

²⁵ Now Elijah said to the prophets of Baal, "Choose one bull for yourselves and prepare it first, for you are many; and call on the name of your god, but put no fire under it."²⁶ So they took the bull which was given them, and they prepared it, and called on the name of Baal from morning even till noon, saying, "O Baal, hear us!" But there was no voice; no one answered. Then they leaped about the altar which they had made.²⁷ And so it was, at noon, that Elijah mocked them and said, "Cry aloud, for he is a god; either he is meditating, or he is busy, or he is on a journey, or perhaps he is sleeping and must be awakened." ²⁸ So they cried aloud, and cut themselves, as was their custom, with knives and lances, until the blood gushed out on them. ²⁹ And when midday was past, they prophesied until the time of the offering of the evening sacrifice. But there was no voice; no one answered, no one paid attention.³⁰ Then Elijah said to all the people, "Come near to me." So, all the people came near to him. And he repaired the altar of the Lord that was broken down. ³¹ And Elijah took twelve stones, according to the number of the tribes of the sons of Jacob, to whom the word of the Lord had come, saying, "Israel shall be your name." [32] Then with the stones he built an altar in the name of the Lord; and he made a trench around the altar large enough to hold two seahs of seed. [33] And he put the wood in order, cut the bull in pieces, and laid it on the wood, and said, "Fill four waterpots with water, and pour it on the burnt sacrifice and on the wood." [34] Then he said, "Do it a second time," and they did It a second time; and he said, "Do it a third time," and they did it a third time. [35] So the water ran all around the altar; and he also filled the trench with water. [36] And it came to pass, at the time of the offering of the evening sacrifice, that Elijah the prophet came near and said, "Lord God of Abraham, Isaac, and Israel, let it be known this day that You are God in Israel, and I am Your servant, and that I have done all these things at Your word. [37] Hear me, O Lord, hear me, that this people may know that You are the Lord God and that You have turned their hearts back to You again." [38] Then the fire of the Lord fell and consumed the burnt sacrifice, and the wood and the stones and the dust, and it licked up the water that was in the trench. [39] Now when all the people saw it, they fell on their faces; and they said, "The Lord, He is God! The Lord, He is God!" [40] And Elijah said to them, "Seize the prophets of Baal! Do not let one of them escape!" So, they seized them; and Elijah brought them down to the Brook Kishon and executed them there.

The discourse on Mt. Carmel resulted in approximately 400 prophets of Baal and others execution this is an example of how far people are willing to go for what they believe. These ancestors who survived the exodus of Egypt and many other documented catastrophes had a different opinion about who the one and only true God is and openly threw themselves on the altar of the god they carried around, displayed in their homes, they washed, and cleaned etcetera. Their god did not hear them let alone answer their prayers. In the demonstration at Mt. Carmel, the prophets of Baal and others witnessed the power and authority of the God of Abraham. Those who worshiped God as demonstrated in this account through Elijah had no doubt the God of Israel would light a blazing fire under the bull and water drenched altar.

Prayer is key when you are praying to God and not idol gods. Prayer helps you to understand and love one another. Prayer is a powerful tool that can move mountains and will help you to see the other person's perspective and show you how to love them. 1 John 3:18, says: *"Dear children, let us not love with words or speech but with actions and in truth,"* you can strive to reach out and love your neighbor, even if you don't agree with them. You can show love and extend an olive branch to your brothers and sisters by having hope and faith in God.

Despite the chaos and turmoil existing in the world, reflect and remind yourself of God's plan for you. You can easily reach out in love to those who may not share the same views as you. 1 Corinthians 13:13, says: *"So now faith, hope, and love abide, these three; but the* greatest of these is love," You can be inspired to practice unconditional love for all and recognize despite our differences, we can still find common ground and love each other. Loving one another despite our differences is a difficult task, and yet it is a challenge you must rise to if you are to build connections and a better world. There are few moral accomplishments more important than this. To help you stay on the path to understanding, there are a few things you must do.

First, you must reach out in love and understanding. You must accept while we may have our differences, we all share the same common humanity. You must recognize the dignity of your neighbor, even if they have beliefs or habits, you do not share. Second, you must dive into your common ancestry. Although you may celebrate different holidays or adhere to different cultures, we all come from the same original source. We are all descended from the same family, and this gives us a common connection we can look back on in order to build a foundation for understanding. Third, you must pray to God. Praying gives you the strength to carry on when your differences seem insurmountable. Praying opens your mind and heart to the beauty of your neighbor's beliefs and help you to pray about the differences that divide you. Finally, you must have hope in God's plan.

God has a purpose for you, and His plan will help you to understand your differences, admit you may be on the same journey, despite your differences. By following these steps, you will learn to love. You can build bridges instead of walls, and create something beautiful out of the diversity in the world. You can overcome the differences that divide you and learn to come together in harmony and peace. Reach out to your neighbors with love and understanding and build a better future together. Though we all are descendants of Adam and Eve whether you want to believe it or not, our ancestors lived in different places, chose different cultures, and backgrounds that is why we look different, speak differently, have different opinions, views, and values. We now know differences of opinions, views, and values can exist right under the roof of your own household. So, you can stop worrying about having raised aliens and stop saying: Who are these people!

In a world of diversity, sometimes it is hard to come together in harmony and peace. However, it is possible to love one another, and it starts with understanding and patience. Learning about each other is the best way to bridge the gap between your diverse backgrounds. Simple tasks like talking to your neighbors or taking the time to learn about a culture other than your own builds understanding. If you show kindness and compassion to those around you, rather than judgement, you can inspire others to do the same.

In times of controversy, it can be especially tempting to stay within your comfort zone and close off from others. Instead, it's important to cast aside your biases and be an ally. Stand up for one another, no matter what differences exist. You can be there to support each other in times of need. Take active steps to come together in peace and acknowledge acceptance is also key. You can start in your own community by joining together for local events that celebrate diversity. These can be anything from art events, festivals, parades, or interfaith gatherings. We are all connected. Whether we live in small towns or large cities, we all share the same planet and it's essential we come together for its future. By learning to love one another, we can all work together to make the world a better place. It's up to you to make the conscious choice to be kind and understanding to those around you. Don't be confused in your thinking or loyalty to God. *"For although they knew God, they did not honor him as God or give thanks to him, but they became futile in their thinking and their foolish hearts were darkened.* [Romans 1:21]

Let's pray for our brothers and sisters who are fighting one another all over the world. Let's pray God will show you how to love one another unconditionally. Let's pray God will help you in your disbelief and pray you will grow compassion to love beyond your judgment parameters and let God guide you. Let's pray for the safety of our innocent infants and children around the world. Do not be stiffed neck with a hardened heart." Meditate and practice what is taught in 1 Corinthians 13: 1-13:

> *13 If I speak in the tongue of men or of angels, but do not have love, I am only a resounding gong or a clanging cymbal. ² If I have the gift of prophecy and can fathom all mysteries and all knowledge, and if I have a faith that can move mountains, but do not have love, I am nothing. ³ If I give all I possess to the poor and give over my body to hardship that I may boast, but do not have love, I gain nothing.⁴ Love is patient, love is kind. It does not envy, it does not boast, it is not proud. ⁵ It does not dishonor others, it is not self-seeking, it is not easily angered, it keeps no record of wrongs. ⁶ Love does not delight in evil but rejoices with the truth. ⁷ It always protects, always trusts, always hopes, always perseveres.⁸ Love never fails. But where there are prophecies, they will cease; where there are tongues, they will be stilled; where there is knowledge, it will pass*

away. ⁹ For we know in part, and we prophesy in part, ¹⁰
but when completeness comes, what is in part disappears.
¹¹ When I was a child, I talked like a child, I thought like
a child, I reasoned like a child. When I became a man, I
put the ways of childhood behind me. ¹² For now we see
only a reflection as in a mirror; then we shall see face to
face. Now I know in part; then I shall know fully, even
as I am fully known.¹³ And now these three remain: faith,
hope and love. But the greatest of these is love.

THIS IS ABOUT YOU

Love your neighbors "For Real." We emphasize "For Real" for a reason. You can be fake. You can grin in a person's face in pretense. In fact, you have perfected the fakeness in your walk and talk. Sometimes to keep the peace and other times because you are waiting for the right time to get the person(s) told. They are not the issue, you are. You can't be real in expressing genuine love if you don't love yourself. Love is a foreign four-letter word to you because you don't know how to love yourself. You simply can't give what you don't have. That's a problem. Typically, people who don't love themselves, end up being a door mat for everyone to walk on because they lack self-esteem and confidence. They are easily bullied and mistreated because they give off a vibe of self-defeat. People who don't love themselves are often looking for someone to love them, but the void is never filled, and they remain unfulfilled because they are looking for validation. They just can't put their finger on the problem that stares back at them in the mirror.

Then there are the selfish people. The ones who are stuck on themselves and there is no room for them to possibly love someone else as much as they loved themselves. That's just not going to happen. If this is your DNA, you are proud, boastful, and not necessarily the best person to judge your own character. You typically think less of other people so you can be elevated above them even if you aren't really above them. This whole conversation about loving your neighbors is about God's command for you to love one another. You do not want people looking down on you, so don't look down on them. You don't want people taking advantage of you, but you take advantage of them. Of course, this is not true across the board for everyone.

I leave you to learn from Apostle Paul's first letter to the Thessalonians in [1 Thessalonians 5:1-26] and to apply it to your life as you learn to love your neighbors as you love yourself.

The Day of the Lord

> *"Now, brothers and sisters, about times and dates we do not need to write to you, ²for you know very well that the day of the Lord will come like a thief in the night.³ While people are saying, "Peace and safety," destruction will come on them suddenly, as labor pains on a pregnant woman, and they will not escape.⁴ But you, brothers, and sisters, are not in darkness so that this day should surprise you like a thief. ⁵ You are all children of the light and children of the day. We do not belong to the night or to the darkness. ⁶ So then, let us not be like others, who*

are asleep, but let us be awake and sober. ⁷ For those who sleep, sleep at night, and those who get drunk, get drunk at night. ⁸ But since we belong to the day, let us be sober, putting on faith and love as a breastplate, and the hope of salvation as a helmet. ⁹ For God did not appoint us to suffer wrath but to receive salvation through our Lord Jesus Christ. ¹⁰ He died for us so that, whether we are awake or asleep, we may live together with him. ¹¹ Therefore encourage one another and build each other up, just as in fact you are doing.

Final Instructions

¹² Now we ask you, brothers, and sisters, to acknowledge those who work hard among you, who care for you in the Lord and who admonish you. ¹³ Hold them in the highest regard in love because of their work. Live in peace with each other. ¹⁴ And we urge you, brothers and sisters, warn those who are idle and disruptive, encourage the disheartened, help the weak, be patient with everyone.¹⁵ Make sure that nobody pays back wrong for wrong, but always strive to do what is good for each other and for everyone else.¹⁶ Rejoice always, ¹⁷ pray continually, ¹⁸ give thanks in all circumstances; for this is God's will for you in Christ Jesus.¹⁹ Do not quench the Spirit. ²⁰ Do not treat prophecies with contempt ²¹ but test them all; hold on to what is good, ²² reject every kind of evil.²³ May God himself, the God of peace, sanctify you through and through. May your whole spirit, soul and body be kept blameless at the coming of our Lord Jesus Christ. [24] The one who calls you is faithful, and he will do it.[25] Brothers and sisters, pray for us. [26] Greet all God's people with a holy kiss. [27] I charge you before the Lord to have this letter read to all the brothers and sisters.[28] The grace of our Lord Jesus Christ be with you."

CHAPTER 27

The Toilet Stool Conversation Remix

The toilet stool ministry is designed to demonstrate how one could be temporarily out of Order. The toilet stool analogy will bring truth to light. Everyone knows what a toilet stool is and what it is used for. Pretty gross to think of it in the context of human life. We deposit stinky things into the toilet. That stench is the waste from our bodies. Stuff that our bodies determined is not needed. Not useful for our health and well-being. Poop and Pee there I said it. It is also a known fact that sometimes like our body systems, the toilet can clog up. Yeah, there's this apparatus called a plunger that can assist us with getting the waste down-forever gone one might say. It will only be a matter of time before it's used again with the expectation it will flush.

No one likes to look in the toilet stool to see all the messy stuff floating to the top for everyone to see. Sort of like the stuff in our life that we want to keep hidden yet all of a sudden it floats to the top, rears its ugly head and everyone sees just who you are. Not the perfect tidy toilet bowl but the crap and stuff. No one likes to clean the toilet bowl either. That's like a job of punishment. luxury is having a toilet brush to clean the inside and not having to use your hands. God forbids! Unlike the toilet bowl you cannot physically reach inside of your body to clean it out. God built a natural way for your body systems to purge and purify. Gross, Gross, and Gross you might say and find a problem with anyone who would take God's loving Words and say them in the same breath as toilet stool. This is not sacrilege!

Our society has a habit of crapping on people who do not meet their highfalutin standards. The toilet stool can be a constant reminder of our daily walk with God. We have to purge some stuff out of our lives like stuff is purged out of our bodies daily. Your body empties out the crap at least two to three times a day if it functions correctly. So, you should have an expectation that it will at least take this amount of time to purge things from your mind, heart, and spirit daily. You know what an overflowing toilet can smell like when poop has set more than we can speak about. Your uniquely made body organs naturally want to get rid of waste. Some of us know all too well what it feels like when our body is clogged up and problems with purging the crap out is painful.

We become constipated, the waste feels hard and big as a brick and there is this tiny little hole it has to come out of. Gross and nasty thoughts and conversation. But it's true. You might be a person that has to rely on external means to get your body plumbing flushed. The point of this gross illustration is that sometimes our lives become like an overflowing toilet stool. Filled with drug and alcohol addiction. Like a full toilet, no one wants to see you coming. They know the stench of this life can cause all sorts of problems.

They know they can't trust an alcoholic or drug addict. Because they lie and manipulate to get their next high. It is not about you it's about the thing they are addicted to that speaks to them at all hours of the night driving them to get whatever it takes to pay for the next high. Paying for the next high with money isn't the disgusting issue. It's paying with your reputation, integrity, credibility, body, mind, heart, and soul that moves the needle up a notch.

It's seeing the faces of your parents who hurt beyond your imagination because they didn't raise you this way and they love you with all of their hearts whatever is left after seeing you throw your life away. What about the toilet stool stench of murder? Taking someone's life because your gut raged with envy and jealousy. Something farting wouldn't cure for you. Your bowels rumble and bubble and overcome you with uncomely thoughts you just can't seem to push out of that tiny hole. So, you seek external remedies to solve your stinking problems. These tiny mentions of the human bodies small attributes are just a glimpse of how our lives can be likened to an overflowing toilet.

The plunger, a device with usually a long wooden handle, and rubber cup is used to clear blocked pipes by means of water pressure. Ironically, doctors instruct you to drink plenty of water to flush your internal systems. We can be so full of crap on a given day and like the need to purge the body systems regularly we need to have an up to the minute on going conversation with God. Of course, there are other sins beyond alcohol and drug addiction. There are those, who have sex and pornography addictions. There are cheaters, liars, backbiters, adulterers, murders, gossipers, manipulators, child abusers, child sex predators, and many other sins that must not go unnoticed or talked about.

They all fall in the purview of crap in the toilet equating to a toilet stool life. Stuff that Sunday morning congregants don't want to hear about. Because we all want to feel good. We don't want to leave church with a rumbling belly that feels like it's about to explode. The toilet stool issue is one that can be managed by caring for the pipes and plumbing on a regular basis, so the system doesn't get clogged to the point of floating elements and the need to call a plumber to come and snake out your system.

God warns you about cluttering your mind, and your heart, with the problems you encounter when you detach yourself from the vine... the lifeline God created for you through the life of his Son, Jesus the Christ. Stench can be smelled from miles away. If you have ever been in the vicinity of a pigpen, cow manure, and horse poop, you get the picture. You can smell the stench on peoples' bodies and breath most times when you are close to them.

What about the people who are filled with stench and crap internally you can't see? in Biblical times lepers were ostracized and separated from the people because people could see their ailments and judge them. While at the same time people who were dressed up in uniforms looking respectable to the eye were filled with crap called hate! bias! lust! greed! and other unpleasing characteristics. They are treated differently because they are able to coverup any noticeable internal stench with their titles, wealth, lifestyle, perfume, and basic soap and water. Things equally respectable homeless people don't have.

The toilet stool life is something that God has an answer for. He wants to introduce you to His Son who came to earth in the body of a man to find you. To meet you just as you are. He came to give you eternal life. A life that would never end if you make the right choice. God wants you to know where you sit, like the toilet stool can be a place of redemption and restoration. God is letting you know in His Word as written in the Bible you don't have to accept a life full of crap. You don't have to be downtrodden.

If you are in that position, it is because you have not gotten up off the toilet stool. The thing is not many bible fearing believers want to meet you where you are especially not on the toilet stool. They would not have wanted to do anything with the woman who had the issue of blood because they would have considered her unclean. But Jesus went everywhere and anywhere to find the lost. He didn't come to save the good smelling righteous people who didn't feel they needed God. Jesus met people where they were as we should. What will it take for God to change your perspective and open your eyes, so you see through a different lens? We have gotten so tired these days because the world has become like a giant toilet stool. People are no longer using the porcelain China bowl to privately release their bowels; they are using the world platforms. Social media and other outlets to crap on people releasing their stench in the atmosphere as they seek to kill and destroy their adversaries whose internal plumbing systems work!

We know we are sick when nothing seems to matter anymore. The name of Jesus is not reverenced even by the people who claim to be his followers. Along with those world leaders who fashion themselves to be God and want to re-write the Bible in an attempt to destroy God's Word. The tower of Babel repeated by different means and methods. Don't be fooled God has never left the throne and his strength and wrath never wails.

This world God created has been purged by God and only those selected persons, animals and insects were saved aboard Noah's Ark. Some people spend quite a bit of time in the bathroom. It could be a perfect place to leave messages of hope and joy. You never know what lost souls might be there looking for answers in the love of Jesus. Are you able to show **JESUS** to them? Perhaps this conversation is unbearable and distasteful for you. You may want to deflate the value of the text by saying well wait a minute, poop and pee don't clog the toilet it's the tissue paper and other things people flush down the toilet that causes the problem.

So, there! Glad you made this observation because it further makes the case, your body systems don't naturally clog up when you use it and treat it like you are supposed to. It's the things you put into it that causes the problems: drugs, alcohol, caffeine, tobacco, vapors, candy-sweets: not going to make a laundry list here but you should get it. It boils down to bad choices you make inclusive of wrong eating habits. I am merely sharing God's viewpoint is perfectly clear. He sees and knows all. He's using me as an instrument to get this message out to you. He has given the traffic signs to illustrate his warnings to you.

He chose to use the words most of us won't admit "Sorry, I am out of order." "Sorry, like this toilet stool, I am out of order." "When I am not working, you can't use me." "I need to be fixed, before the sign will be taken down to signify, I am back in working order." "All pipes and equipment have been flushed and cleaned. I have been restored usable."

God uses who He chooses. Accept God's choices and continue to support the ministry as a humble and obedient servant of God. Flush your toilet and get the work done!

CHAPTER 28

> ## OUT OF SERVICE FOR REPAIRS

Out of Service for Repairs: Fixing Our Broken Lives

It's a familiar sight in most households: appliances that don't work need repairs. We've all seen the signs that say, 'Out of Service for Repairs'. However, these signs can also be applied to your broken life. Sometimes you need to be fixed or repaired. Sometimes your life can be complicated and messy. You get overwhelmed or become emotionally and physically drained. Just like a broken appliance, you need to be out of service for repairs. You must prioritize your wellbeing and understand it is alright to take a break from the things stressing you out. In other words, it's okay to slow down and take a break from life now and then.

Good news, the Bible tells you, no matter how broken you may be, God is always there to help you. *"I know the plans I have for you,"* declares the Lord, *"plans to prosper you and not to harm you, plans to give you hope and a future."* [Jeremiah 29:11]. This means that no matter how broken you may feel, there is hope. God wants you to rely on Him and He will restore [repair] you. When you are out of service for repairs, trust God hugs you even tighter and makes you whole again. Take comfort He will heal you.

With God's help, no situation is too difficult for you to face. So, if you find yourself in need of repairs – be it for an appliance or your life – know God is with you. Lean on Him and allow Him to carry the burden for you. For those who Feel Broken Down and In Need of Repairs but don't feel close to God or perhaps you don't even know Him, we've all been there. Many people have felt down, discouraged, and in desperate need of a good repair and tune-up. Life can leave you feeling like a broken-down car in need of a mechanic, an appliance in need of a technician, or a life in need of an overhaul. But what if you were told there was a better kind of repair available? What if you were offered permanent repair and solution? What if, instead of being stuck in a long wait at the repair shop, you could be renewed and refreshed in an instant? [figuratively speaking—there's no magical poof-but there are miracles]

The good news of the gospel—God has promised to renew and refresh the innermost parts of your heart and life. No matter how far off course you've wandered, He is faithful to meet you where you are and lead you back home. The best part is, He doesn't need to send you out for service or repairs. He doesn't need to take you apart and put you back together again. He simply fills you up with His loving presence and peace. You are restored, made completely new [confessing your sins and repentance is required].

When you feel like you're in need of a complete overhaul, remember Jesus is with you, ready to carry the burden for you. Lean on Him and allow Him to make the repair. He is the one who will give you true hope and peace in the midst of life's heavy and difficult times. You must not be wishy washy, double-minded, or afraid. You must trust and believe. God's repair is the best kind of repair you can hope for. So, when life's troubles start to weigh you down or you feel like you're in need of repairs, get out the way and let God. Lean on Him and allow Him to repair you and give you the renewal you need.

Out of Service for Repairs: A Guide to Renewal with God We all struggle from time to time. Life can be tough and even the most resilient of us need a break. Unfortunately, there are times where we can feel like we are completely "out of service, drained of energy and enthusiasm. If this is the case, don't worry, pray, and ask God for deliverance. Tell God all about your struggles and mishaps. He already knows everything but don't take that for granted. Pour out your heart to Him and tell Him what you want. You don't have to be fancy or sugarcoat anything. Go to God with a pure heart. God has always been there for you, even in your darkest hours. He is always willing to lend you a helping hand and guide you through your problems. When it comes to "Out of Service for Repairs," He is the best mechanic from here to eternity. Trust Him and His word. He will make sure you run at full capacity again in good health with a sound mind!

You may be a person who says, "I did all of that. I prayed, fasted, and ran around the block a few times. I even gave up most of my vices and sins. I felt good for a little while and then life started happening again. I found myself worn out again." If you feel worn out and in need of replenishing again, stay in communication with God, tell Him. You don't have to be in church to do so. God is with you no matter where you are. Talk to Him like never before. Unload all of your worries and anxieties and allow Him to take care of them. He will listen, understand, and provide you with the solace and comfort you need. Be sure to attend church and get involved in fellowship with other believers as often as possible. This is a great way to stay connected with God and to get a sense of renewal and restoration. Also, be sure to read your bible daily and meditate on His Word. This will provide you with the spiritual sustenance needed to repair the broken places in your heart and your mind.

Let's make sure you noticed the person quoted above gave up most of their vices and sins...not all of them. You should expect trouble when you try to straddle the fence between God and Satan. Of course, you will find yourself back in the old movie of your life because you held on to the drama and perhaps like the sensation of trouble. Be careful you are playing with fire, and you might get burned.

Remember to take spiritual action in your life. Allow the Holy Spirit to do His mighty work in and through you. Do not allow the Comforter Jesus left to dwell with you—inside you permanently lay dormant in your life un-activated! Take practical steps the Holy Spirit gives you to get back on track. Pray for guidance and then make a plan to carry out the changes you need to make to stay on track. You will not be able to do this without God. When life's troubles start to weigh you down or you feel like you're in need of repairs, remember God's promises and meditate on them. Lean on Him and allow Him to bring you the repairs and renewal you need. Trust, He will provide you with all the tools you need to move forward and live a life of abundance and joy. So go forth and "get to work" with God, you will soon find yourself back in service with a smile on your face!

CHAPTER 29

Prayer Changes You Before Things

Prayer has been a great source of strength and power for many throughout history, and it is no surprise it is a central theme in the Bible. Throughout the Bible, you find numerous examples of how prayer has been used to communicate and receive support from God. We will take an in-depth look at the various Bible passages that discuss prayer, and also provide some examples where God answered prayers.

The Bible portrays prayer as a vital part of a relationship with God. In the book of Luke, you are *told "men ought always to pray, and not to faint"* (Luke 18:1 KJV). You must pray continually to accomplish God's Will for your life. The widow who wanted God to avenge her of her adversary was persistent. She was not going to stop until her prayer was answered. This passage should ignite a fire in you to be persistent in prayer this is an important part of your life, and God listens when you call out to Him.

How bad do you want what you want? You want to find a man to marry despite Proverbs 18:22 *"Whoso findeth a wife findeth a good thing, and obtaineth favor of the Lord."* We know you want to help God because you don't think He will give you the man of your dreams. You know one who fits your descriptive list of the physical attributes he must possess, "Tall, dark, and handsome with riveting muscles and a dazzling smile. Whatever your cup of tea is or the flavor you dream of you don't really want to trust God because you are afraid, He's not going to get it right. Some women don't agree the man will find them on his own. So, you might take matters into your own hands.

As long as the heat of the moment lasts and you feel like you lassoed your man into marriage, you are good until it's not so good. You begin to see differently. He's not what you thought he would be. All of a sudden you discover you picked the man by yourself and expected God to bless your pick. If you are a man, you are in the same shoes. You allowed your flesh to choose a woman for You. Your little head controlled your big head. Translation: the big head is the one with the brain and the little head is the one with the sperm. It doesn't work out the way you envisioned when you no longer feel the same way about the woman your little head chose for you. The big head awakens! Your mind wandered elsewhere when you discovered you settled and didn't really find the right one. Answered prayer doesn't measure up to a mistake. God doesn't make MISTAKES. You should pray and ask God about the wife you think you found before you get intimately involved and married.

Remember Satan has tricks laid out for you. He does not want you to find a Christian woman, and make Christian babies. He wants you to help him trick other people into his lair of pain and misery. You lack of control and discipline can unleash havoc on the world. The children you abandon when you no longer have eyes for their mother are left in despair. They do not know where to place the blame or guilt. Most times they blame themselves for the cause of your breakup. In what seems like a blink of the eye to them their family has been destroyed. The adults put temporary Band-Aids on the kids wounds and try to keep it moving. Kids act out, rebel, tired of being hoisted between two households [halted between two different opinions] on the weekends, summers, and in between. They feel discarded and unwanted by both parents.

Girls want to know why their daddy abandoned them when he said he loved them and would always protect them. Some of them grow up looking for a daddy figure in a man. They try to fill a void their boyfriend or husband can never fill. God can fill the void. But more than likely she won't ask God because she's angry with God too. After all, from her point of view, God destroyed her family. Boys often suffer too. They are left in the home to pick up the pieces. They love their mother's so much they can't forgive their father for abandoning her. Some mothers replace their husband with their sons. [Not intimately] They tell them they are the man of the house and have to protect the family. Can you imagine tossing this huge responsibility on a ten-year-old boy? His first hero was his father and now he finds his hero was nothing more than a piece of you know what. Many children are living a wounded discarded life, and they don't know how to pick up the pieces.

They feel labeled and insecure. Forced to be in the middle of their parent's drama feeling like they have to pick and choose which one they love best. It's not easy for kids to accept mommy found a new man and begins to have his children. Often time the new man is only interested in their mother and the children he have with her. The experience for them is the same when their father takes a new wife, or woman and have additional children. Children feel like they have been replaced by a new family and some feel completely erased. People talk about extended and blended families but it's not as easy as it looks or sounds.

If you, the man, were a praying man, who depends on God for every decision you make, you will experience pleasurable outcomes. The Proverbs 31 woman could have been your wife if you had sought the bible for guidance. King Lemuel's mother did not want her son to choose a woman unbefitting for a King. She wanted him to choose wisely so she gave him Godly counsel. This is interesting because men today, think they must detach themselves from their mother's apron strings and separate themselves from the one woman who knows everything about them and from whom they can receive great counsel before they get married.

Here's what King Lemuel's mother shared with her beloved son as she counseled him on how to be a man of good character and how to find and recognize a virtuous woman:

[Proverbs 31: 1-31]

> *The sayings of King Lemuel—an inspired utterance his mother taught him.² Listen, my son! Listen, son of my womb! Listen, my son, the answer to my prayers!³ Do not spend your strength on women, your vigor on those who ruin kings.⁴ It is not for kings, Lemuel— it is not for*

kings to drink wine, not for rulers to crave beer[5] lest they drink and forget what has been decreed, and deprive all the oppressed of their rights.[6] Let beer be for those who are perishing, wine for those who are in anguish![7] Let them drink and forget their poverty and remember their misery no more.[8] Speak up for those who cannot speak for themselves, for the rights of all who are destitute.[9] Speak up and judge fairly; defend the rights of the poor and needy.

Epilogue: The Wife of Noble Character

[10] A wife of noble character who can find? She is worth far more than rubies.[11] Her husband has full confidence in her and lacks nothing of value.[12] She brings him good, not harm, all the days of her life.[13] She selects wool and flax and works with eager hands.[14] She is like the merchant ships, bringing her food from afar.[15] She gets up while it is still night; she provides food for her family and portions for her female servants.[16] She considers a field and buys it; out of her earnings she plants a vineyard.[17] She sets about her work vigorously; her arms are strong for her tasks.[18] She sees that her trading is profitable, and her lamp does not go out at night. [19] In her hand she holds the distaff and grasps the spindle with her fingers.[20] She opens her arms to the poor and extends her hands to the needy.[21] When it snows, she has no fear for her household,

for all of them are clothed in scarlet.²² She makes coverings for her bed; she is clothed in fine linen and purple.²³ Her husband is respected at the city gate, where he takes his seat among the elders of the land.²⁴ She makes linen garments and sells them, and supplies the merchants with sashes.²⁵ She is clothed with strength and dignity; she can laugh at the days to come.²⁶ She speaks with wisdom, and faithful instruction is on her tongue.²⁷ She watches over the affairs of her household and does not eat the bread of idleness.²⁸ Her children arise and call her blessed her husband also, and he praises her:²⁹ "Many women do noble things, but you surpass them all."³⁰ Charm is deceptive, and beauty is fleeting; but a woman who fears the Lord is to be praised.³¹ Honor her for all that her hands have done, and let her works bring her praise at the city gate.

I must admit, a Proverbs 31 woman sets the bar high and is intimidating to every woman who aspires to be a Proverbs 31 woman. I spent years trying to measure up to the standards outlined in these verses. I am still a work in progress. A Proverbs 31-woman is no joke and she's hard to find. The little head would never take the time to find her. King Lemuel's mother lovingly told her **son "Charm is deceptive, and beauty is fleeting; but a woman who fears the Lord is to be praised."** [Proverbs 31:30] If a man finds a Proverbs 31 woman he finds much! Don't let the woman deceive you with her looks, talent, money. Body, sex, or any other womanly devices. A mature man, [not a child] who is in control of his faculties and disciplined will not allow his little head to make lifelong decisions for him. He is a God-fearing man not to be tricked by the wiles of the devil and what lies between a woman's legs.

Woman if you are seeking a man, pray and position yourself rightly rooted in the Word of God and your knight in shining armor will find you. You must trust God. God does not need your help; you need His help so listen to His instructions and follow them. Marriage is a covenant you and your spouse enter into with God. No man or woman is able to penetrate this bond or put it asunder! The promise is through the good and bad times and through sickness and health and through financial hardships and woes. It's not I found something better, more pleasing to my eyesight and loins. A Jezebel spirit lurks around every corner and doorstep looking for her prey. Man or woman, it doesn't matter to this corrupting spirit she will turn you out quicker than you can sneeze and leave you defeated on your knees. Don't disregard the wise counsel of your mother or father who truly loves you and demonstrates this throughout your life.

Woman choose a God-fearing man God sends to you. Stop going after eye candy you know will turn from sweet to sour as each day passes not so for the man God sends. You reject God's choice because you don't want what's best for you, you want what someone else has, not necessarily their man but one like theirs. You should not be naïve and allow the devil to throw any man your way because you are horny and desperate. Wait, I say on the Lord. "*The Lord is good to those who wait for Him, To the person who seeks Him.* [Lamentations 3:25]

You also find in 1 Thessalonians 5:17 "*pray without ceasing*" (KJV). You should know prayer is not something that should be done only when problems arise, but should be an ongoing part of your life.

One thing you should know about asking people to pray with you and for you, they may start praying but may not finish or they may fall asleep and not pray at all. Jesus asked his disciples to watch and pray at a critical point in his life when betrayal was afoot, and His death was near. Jesus went off to pray and they went to sleep.

> "*38 Then saith he unto them, My soul is exceeding sorrowful, even unto death: tarry ye here, and watch with me.39 And he went a little farther, and fell on his face, and prayed, saying, O my Father, if it be possible, let this cup pass from me: nevertheless, not as I will, but as thou wilt.40 And he cometh unto the disciples, and findeth them asleep, and saith unto Peter, What, could ye not watch with me one hour?41 Watch and pray, that ye enter not into temptation: the spirit indeed is willing, but the flesh is weak.42 He went away again the second time, and prayed, saying, O my Father, if this cup may not pass away from me, except I drink it, thy will be done.43 And he came and found them asleep again: for their eyes were heavy.44 And he left them, and went away again, and prayed the third time, saying the same words.*"
> [Matthew 26:38-44]

It's a sad message, but we know people are well intentioned. Our need doesn't always translate as their need and if they don't pray for themselves, it's not likely they will really pray for you. Don't get disgruntled, handle your business, and pray for yourself. You will know without a doubt

God heard your prayers. Pray for others as God has commanded and don't worry about reciprocal prayers.

The Bible contains various examples of how God answered prayers. In Exodus 34: 27-28 God heard the prayers of Moses and answered them in the form of the Ten Commandments.

> *"27 And the Lord said unto Moses, Write thou these words: for after the tenor of these words I have made a covenant with thee and with Israel.28 And he was there with the Lord forty days and forty nights; he did neither eat bread, nor drink water. And he wrote upon the tables the words of the covenant, the ten commandments."*

In 1 Kings 3, you get an opportunity to see how valuable and important it is for children to listen to their parent's instructions. Solomon showed his love for the Lord by walking according to his father, David's instructions. Except he offered sacrifices and burned incense on the high places. In comparison, perhaps both Cain and Abel were given important instructions from their parents Adam and Eve but only Abel operated according to their instructions and gave God generously more. His brother on the other hand, held back part of his offering to God. Hence, they experienced different outcomes. Back to Solomon. Solomon formed an alliance with Pharaoh the King of Egypt, and he married his daughter. Both the King and Solomon offered sacrifices at Gibeon which was the most important high place. [Not saying they did their offerings at the same time or together]. While Solomon was at Gibeon the Lord appeared to him at night in a dream. *"God said to him, "Ask for whatever you want me to give you."* [1Kings 3:5]

Solomon's Ask:

⁶ Solomon answered, "You have shown great kindness to your servant, my father David, because he was faithful to you and righteous and upright in heart. You have continued this great kindness to him and have given him a son to sit on his throne this very day.

⁷ "Now, Lord my God, you have made your servant king in place of my father David. But I am only a little child and do not know how to carry out my duties. ⁸ Your servant is here among the people you have chosen, a great people, too numerous to count or number. ⁹ So give your servant a discerning heart to govern your people and to distinguish between right and wrong. For who is able to govern this great people of yours?" [1 Kings 3:6-9]

God's Answer to Solomon:

¹⁰ The Lord was pleased that Solomon had asked for this.¹¹ So God said to him, "Since you have asked for this and not for long life or wealth for yourself, nor have asked for the death of your enemies but for discernment in administering justice, ¹² I will do what you have asked. I will give you a wise and discerning heart, so that there will never have been anyone like you, nor will there ever be. ¹³ Moreover, I will give you what you have not asked for—both wealth and honor—so that in your lifetime you will have no equal among kings. ¹⁴ And if you walk in obedience to me and keep my decrees and commands as David your father did, I will give you a long life."¹⁵ Then Solomon awoke—and he realized it had been a dream.

[1Kings 3:10-15]

If you didn't believe it before or felt you needed proof that God answers prayers, now you have it. Solomon prayed for wisdom and understanding, and God granted his requests. How many times has God spoke to you and asked you to ask of him whatever you wanted? Consider God's promise in Mark 11: 22-26:

"²² "Have faith in God," Jesus answered. ²³ "Truly I tell you, if anyone says to this mountain, 'Go, throw yourself into the sea,' and does not doubt in their heart but believes that what they say will happen, it will be done for them. ²⁴ Therefore I tell you, whatever you ask for in prayer, believe that you have received it, and it will be yours. ²⁵ And when you stand praying, if you hold anything against anyone, forgive them, so that your Father in heaven may forgive you your sins."

Stop soaking and telling people God does not hear you and does not answer your prayers. Perhaps He answered and said "No." Maybe He said wait. Maybe He said Yes. If you don't believe God has answered you at all, then pray for clarity and understanding. Be in right status like Solomon worshipping and praising God and honoring God with your first fruits. Trust God, He does not break His promises.

God answered Daniel's prayers and protected him from harm. Daniel understood the Word of God given to Jeremiah. He knew the desolation of Jerusalem would last seventy years. Knowing this, Daniel turned to the Lord God and pleaded with Him in prayer and petition. Daniel fasted in sackcloth and ashes. He prayed and Confessed to God. Daniel 9: 1-19 gives specific details of Daniel's prayer. In verses 20-27 Daniel received an answer to his prayers. The answer may not have been what Daniel expected but God gave him clarity and understanding.

Jesus Prays

You know if Jesus prays, He knows how important it is to stay in communication with God the Father, at all times. There are roughly 29 Bible verses where Jesus prayed. Jesus, the Son of God understands the struggle you have with your flesh, He knows the desires of your flesh will destroy you if you don't pray. Many of Jesus' prayers are recorded in the book of Matthew. *"Ordering the people to sit down on the grass, He took the five loaves and the two fish, and looking up toward heaven, He blessed the food, and breaking the loaves He gave them to the disciples, and the disciples gave them to the crowds."* [Matthew 14:19] In this verse, Jesus fed a multitude of people off of five loaves of bread and two fish. He blessed the food by praying and the disciples distributed the food to the crowds. *"²⁰ They all ate and were satisfied, and the disciples picked up twelve basketfuls of broken pieces that were left over. ²¹ The number of those who ate was about five thousand men, besides women and children."* [Matthew 14:20]

Jesus fed five thousand men, women, and children off of five loaves of bread and two fish and there was twelve basketfuls of broken pieces left over. How many times have you avoided opportunities to invite someone over to break bread with them and fellowship with them? Have you avoided inviting people to your home because you believed you didn't have enough food for everyone? Fellowshipping with others can be fun and an opportunity to share the gift of salvation.

In Matthew 14: 23 Jesus prayed for the crowd after He sent them away: *After He had sent the crowds away, He went up on the mountain by Himself to pray; and when it was evening, He was there alone."* In Matthew 19:13 the disciples rebuked children brought to Jesus, *"Then some children were brought to Him so He might lay His hands on them and pray; and the disciples rebuked those that brought them.*

In Matthew 26:36, *"Then Jesus came with them to a place called Gethsemane, and 'said to his disciples, "Sit here while I go over there and pray. [also in Mark 14:32]* In verse 39 Jesus feeling overwhelmed to the point of death asked Peter and the two sons of Zebedee to stay and keep watch while he prayed: *"And He went a little beyond them, and fell on His face and prayed, saying, "My Father, if it is possible, let this cup pass from Me: Yet, not as I will, but as You will."* [Also, in Mark 14:35] In verse 40 Jesus warns them to pray so they would not fall into temptation: ***"40** Then he returned to his disciples and found them sleeping. "Couldn't you men keep watch with me for one hour?" he asked Peter. **41** "Watch and pray so that you will not fall into temptation. The spirit is willing, but the flesh is weak."*

It is a shame you don't take time to pray for one hour. You might not even spend fifteen minutes praying for yourself let alone your friends and enemies. You don't always take prayer seriously to the level you should. Prayers should not be superficial. Get to know God for yourself and pray without ceasing. In verse 42, Jesus prayed again: *"He went away again a second time and prayed 'saying My Father, if this cannot pass away unless I drink it. Your will be done." And Jesus left them again, and went away and prayed a third time, saying the same thing once more."* [Also, in Mark 14:39]

Jesus prays on your behalf, *"I ask on their behalf, I do not ask on behalf of the world, but of those whom you have given Me; for they are yours."* [John 17:9] *"I do not ask on behalf of these alone, but for those also who believe in Me through their word."* [John 17:20] Jesus prays for your strength and faith, *"but I have prayed for you, that your faith may not fail, and you, when once you have turned again, strengthen your brothers."* [Luke 22:32] Prayer is a powerful weapon, tool, and asset; however, it is a two-edged sword. Be careful what you pray for. You may use prayer to pray against people, weaponizing your words but just as you pray this way know there are others who may be praying for your demise. Thank God for Jesus unselfish prayers. Jesus' prayers for love, faith, and strength on your behalf protects you. Learn to separate yourself from others like Jesus did and pray without ceasing. Remember Jesus said when you gain strength, strengthen your brothers.

Jesus lives [eternally] to intercede for You. Yes You! *"Therefore, He is able also to save forever those who draw near to God through Him since He always lives to make intercession for them."* [Hebrews 7:25] Jesus confidently solidifies your relationship with God, Martha acknowledged this after Jesus raised her brother Lazarus from the dead: *"Even now I know that whatever you ask of God, God will give You."* [John 11:22] In other words, when Jesus prays for you, you know his prayers are the ultimate "hook up." It gets no better than that. Jesus prays, and ask God on your behalf, God will give Jesus whatever He ask for. God in Mark 11:22-24 will give you whatever you ask for in faith without doubt.

When Jesus died on the cross for your sins, He did not die an eternal death. Jesus spoke to God on His death bed, *"Jesus spoke these things, and lifting up His eyes to heaven, He said, 'Father the hour has come; glorify Your Son, that the Son may glorify You, even as You gave Him authority over all flesh, that to all whom You have given Him, He may give eternal life. This is eternal life, that they may know You, the only true God, and Jesus Christ whom You have sent. I have brought you glory on earth by finishing the work you gave me to do. And now, Father, glorify me in your presence with the glory I had with you before the world began."* [Read John 17:1-25]

Jesus has given you a template for your prayers. If you are still confused about what to say and how to say it, you are not the first one who has felt this way. While Jesus was praying one of his disciples asked Him to teach them how to pray just as John taught his disciples. [Luke 11:1]

Jesus Answer:

> *² He said to them, "When you pray, say:*

"'Father,
hallowed be your name,
your kingdom come.
³ Give us each day our daily bread.

⁴ Forgive us our sins,

for we also forgive everyone who sins against us.

And lead us not into temptation."

There are numerous scriptures referring to prayer and how you communicate with God through them. In Philippians 4:6-7, you are told: *"Do not be anxious about anything, but in every situation, by prayer and petition, with thanksgiving, present your requests to God. 7 And the peace of God, which transcends all understanding, will guard your hearts and your minds in Christ Jesus."* This means you should come to God with your concerns and thanksgiving.

In James 5:16, we find, *"Therefore confess your sins to each other and pray for each other so that you may be healed. The prayer of a righteous person is powerful and effective."* You may have heard it this way: "the effective, fervent prayer of a righteous man avails much" (NKJV). The power of prayer is amplified when we are in right standing with God. In 1 John 5:14-15, we find *"if we ask anything according to His will, He hears us." And if we know that He hears us, whatever we ask, we know that we have the petitions that we have asked of Him"* (NKJV). When you pray according to God's will, your prayers will be answered. Surely you have discovered by now prayer is your life, your communication and lifeline to God, and assurance you will receive support from God.

You must take time to study God's living Word. Understand God's lessons on prayer. You must utilize the power of prayer in your own life. Prayer has the ability to change you for the better, and the nonsense in your life no matter the situation. The toilet stool life you want to rid yourself of is a prayer away. The traffic jams in your life keep popping up like rag weeds are demolished by your prayers. Pray with an open heart and a desire to grow closer to God, you will see a shift in your circumstances. You will recognize the changes seen in your life and in the world around you as proof of God's power.

Pay attention to how prayer changes your thoughts and feelings. You will feel the presence of God and comfort of His Spirit. Prayer is a powerful tool that brings about real and lasting transformation to your life. The saying "Prayer Changes Things" is true but more accurately, **prayer changes you and when you change things change.** If you take time to understand God's teachings on prayer, you will optimize its power in your own life. Prayer is a direct line of communication between God and you, it is also a way for you to show gratitude to God for what he has already given and done for you.

Tips on How to Pray

First and foremost, remember Jesus taught us how to pray. We discussed this earlier. These tips are additional pointers for those still struggling with their prayer life and for those who may have become bored with how they pray. When it comes to prayer, there is no one "right" way to pray. However, there are some common tips that can help you make the most of your time in prayer. Here are a few tips on how to pray:

- Take the time to be still and quiet before you pray.
- Acknowledge who God is.
- Express your desire to be close to God.
- Express your needs and wants to God.
- Express thanksgiving and gratitude to God.

- Don't worry about getting the "right" words. Just talk to God as if you're speaking with a good friend.
- End your prayer with "Amen".

You know now prayer is an essential part of your relationship with God. It is a way for you to express your needs, wants, and desires to God and to hear his response to your prayers. By making prayer a part of your daily routine, you will experience true transformation in your life and see lasting change. "Pray without ceasing" (1 Thessalonians 5:17). This means you should be in constant communication with God. Whether it's when you wake up in the morning, before meals, when you are going through difficult times, or just want to express your gratitude, prayer is an amazing way of serving your Lord. Every time you pray, you build a stronger relationship with Him. You open your soul so God can fill you with His power.

Don't forget to confess your sins and shortcomings, ask for His guidance, and seek protection and forgiveness. If you want to experience the true power of prayer and see lasting change, you must make it a part of your daily routine. Prayer changes you and your clear vision and outlook changes things—your perspective. When you connect with God, your life is filled with His peace and His power. Your Prayers change you.

If you are one of those skeptical people pray every now and then only when you want something right then and there from God, you are playing this sort of game where you aren't fully invested but you just want to know if God is real or if he really answers prayers. On top of what has just been said, you want to use the fact God didn't give you what you wanted and, in your opinion, He didn't answer your prayers so you can tell people God doesn't hear you or answer you. You have to believe God loves you. You have to pray with belief. You have to pray with faith. Don't approach God by simply playing games "of what if or will He?" Get to know God. Just be yourself. Tell Him you have doubt. Tell Him you don't really know how to pray if that's the case. Two words that work together are trust and believe.

Heavenly Father, help me. I don't know how to pray. I don't know how to tell you want I really want. There is so much going on in my life and I don't know what to do about all of the stuff. I want to trust you. I want to believe Jesus is your Son who died on the cross for me. I don't understand why he would die for me. I am nobody. I want to let my guard down. I know I can't control everything and be in charge of everything. My life spirals out of control in ways I am ashamed of. Help me. Help me through my unbelief and these dark times. Help me to trust you. Help me when I don't know what to say and what to ask. Do I need to say anything else? Do I say Amen? God help me.

Maybe this prayer reflects who you are right now in your life. Maybe you feel awkward and don't feel worthy of God's love. But if you read this section on Prayer, you know God is real, and he answers your prayers.

Father God, I can't go out like this. I have been worshipping and serving you for a long time. I have prayed many prayers. Some answered and unanswered. I have been serving in church to the point I am tired. I am tired of all of the church stuff and politics. I am tired of being over worked and not validated by the people in my church. I feel like I am just being used. I am so tired. This world according to the news reports has gotten worse. I can't bear to hear about the wars, senseless killings, lootings, and other bad news reports. I am trying to stay focused. I am trying to hold my head up to be a beacon light to others. This journey has been long. I pray you will strengthen and keep me. Help me in my time of need. Bless my Pastor and his family. Keep us safe. In Jesus name, Amen.

CHAPTER 30

Emergency exit is defined as: a designated way out of a building or vehicle, to be used for escape in the event of an emergency. When considering emergency exit signs, it is important to remember God provides emergency exits and escapes for those whom He loves. There are several examples of this throughout the Bible, from the great escape of the Israelites from Egypt to the miraculous deliverance of Shadrach, Meshach, and Abednego from the fiery furnace. In each instance, God provided a way out for those He loved.

In Isaiah 43:2, God tells His people He will make a way for them in the wilderness and rivers in the desert,

> *"But now, this is what the LORD says: he who created you, Jacob, he who formed you, Israel: Do not fear, for I have redeemed you; When you pass through the waters, I will be with you; and when you pass through the rivers,*

they will not sweep over you. When you walk through the fire, you will not be burned; the flames will not set you ablaze."

In Exodus 14:13, God guides the Israelites through the Red Sea in the midst of their enemies.

We are reminded that God fights for us.

> *"And Moses said unto the people, Fear ye not, stand still, and see the salvation of the LORD, which he will shew to you today: for the Egyptians who ye have seen today, ye shall see them no more forever."*

In Psalm 91:14-16, God's promise of safety and provision is made evident in the following verses: *"Because he hath set his love upon me, therefore will I deliver him: I will set him on high, because he hath known my name. He shall call upon me, and I will answer him: I will be with him in trouble; I will deliver him, and honor him. With long life will I satisfy him, and show him my salvation."*

God's emergency exits are reminders of His loving care and protection for you. Take comfort in knowing God will provide the means and guidance so you will make it through any difficult situation. Although it may not be so obvious to you in the moment, looking back on your life you can clearly see the evidence of God's hand in your emergency exits. As you look to the Bible for guidance and understanding, you will know the truth and be rest assured He will continue to provide a way out for you.

From the very first emergency exit sign, which directed Adam and Eve to flee the Garden of Eden when the Lord expelled them from their home for disobedience, to the Passover story in which God directed the Israelites on the right path out of Egypt, to the countless times God has been your refuge and strength, He has never failed to provide a way out for those who rely on Him.

Jeremiah 29:11 says, *"For I know the plans I have for you,' declares the Lord, 'plans to prosper you and not to harm you, plans to give you hope and a future."* In the same way, emergency exit signs lead those in danger to safety, God leads you through your struggles and hardships to a better place. The next time you see an emergency exit sign, remember to thank God for providing a way of escape. Even when you feel lost and helpless, He will never leave your side. He has already provided a way out and will not forsake you. When you keep your faith in Him, He will lead you on the path of safety and security

Emergency exit signs also provide an opportunity to affirm your faith in God. If you have ever had to get out of a situation or a pickle, you know how important it is to get out. You may not know where the emergency exit is or how to get out, but you know God will reveal it to you. Emergency exit signs provide you with physical direction and also with spiritual hope in moments of confusion and fear.

Before take-off, airline stewards point out the emergency exits and give instructions to the passengers how to locate them. Some people are fortunate to be seated directly in front of an emergency exit. God provides emergency exits as well and provides detailed instructions on how to escape the devil's snares and hell. How to escape a sinful life and exchange it for eternal life. He helps you to get out of Harm's way. He provides you an escape plan out of an abusive marriage or relationship. He provided a way for believers to escape the massacre of first-born sons when Pharaoh gave instructions to kill them all. God provided an escape route across the Red Sea when he parted it for the Israelites safe passage.

He provided an escape to the men on the boat when he calmed the winds and subdued the storm. God provided an escape for man and living creatures from the 40 days of nonstop rain that killed everyone and every living creature except those on Noah's Ark. These are examples of emergency exits God provides to help you to get out of harm's way. Yes, He provided an emergency exist where you escaped death. If you think back over your life, you may remember some of the safety routes and emergency exits God provided for you. Some of us would not be here if it were not for God.

CHAPTER 31

Lost And Found:
Eternal Life Is Your Gift

Be diligent find the lost

> *"If a shepherd has a hundred sheep, and one of them has gone astray, does he not leave the ninety-nine on the mountains and go in search of the one that went astray? And if he finds it, truly I tell you, he rejoices over it more than over the ninety-nine that never went astray."*
> [Matthew 18:10-14]

"Now the tax collectors and sinners were all drawing near to him. 2 and the Pharisees and the scribes grumbled, saying, 'This man receives sinners and eats with them.' 3 So he told them this parable: 4 "What man of you, having a hundred sheep, if he has lost one of them, does not leave the ninety-nine in the open-country, and go after the one that is lost, until he finds it? 5 And when he has found it, he lays it on his shoulders, rejoicing. 6 And when he comes home, he calls together his friends and his neighbors, saying to them, 'Rejoice with me, for I have found my sheep that was lost.' 7 Just so, I tell you, there will be more joy in heaven over one sinner who repents than over ninety-nine righteous persons who need no repentance." [Luke 15:3-7]

The reference to sheep by Jesus in these passages of scripture refer to man. Jesus told this parable to help those who drew near to Him to understand how important property and possessions can be to man. He points out the significance of how men feel when they lose something. Their adrenaline race in thought as to where the lost sheep may have gone. They ponder on it to the point of action. Man will leave all of his sheep in the open country to find the lost one. The scripture doesn't say he worried about what could or would happen to the ninety-nine he left grazing in the pasture alone. The lost one was the object of his quest, and he was not going to return until he found the lost one. We further see when he found the one lost sheep he rejoiced and had a celebration because all of his sheep were together again. [too bad today some men don't do that for their children]

I don't know if you have ever lost anything. If you have ever lost money, you probably retraced your steps trying to recall everything you did and every place you went. You searched all of your pockets, your purse, dresser drawers, your usual hiding places and everywhere you could think about to find your money. The thought probably never leaves your mind until you find it or give up looking. Jesus speaks about a woman who lost her money:

> **8** *Or what woman, having ten silver coins, if she loses one coin, does not light a lamp, and sweep the house diligently until she finds it?* **9** *And when she has found it, she calls together her friends and neighbors, saying, 'Rejoice with me, for I have found the coin that I had lost.'* **10** *Just so, I tell you, there is joy before the angels of God over one sinner who repents."* [Luke 15:8-10]

I recall giving one of my younger brothers, three dollars to go to Burger King, on Grand River, near Forrer St. years ago, in Detroit to get us something to eat. I was a little concerned about him crossing Grand River. He told me about all the times he successfully crossed the street on his own, Yada-Yada. I caved gave him the money and when time had passed and he had not returned, I grew concerned. Finally, I took off toward Grand River. As I walked down the street, I saw my brother walking back and forth. He was retracing his steps. When I approached him, tears streamed from his eyes, "I lost the money" He said. He wiggled his fingers through the hole in his pocket and we never found the three dollars, luckily, I had a few more dollars and we got food from Burger King anyway.

Imagine the joy you feel when you find the money you lost or misplaced. Think about how you feel when you can't find the money and you never find it. Something in the back of your mind causes you to keep thinking about it, days, weeks, and even months later. Just like the man who ventured to find his lost sheep, his property, what was his, you'd do the same for your earthly possessions.

But what about people you know and are close to that don't Know Jesus? Those you know who are spiritually lost? Your father, mother, sister, brother, relatives, friends, and colleagues? Are their souls not precious to you as your money and possessions? Are you willing to allow people you love to spend eternity in hell just because you won't open your saved mouth to tell them about Jesus? Man is lost when he is separated from Jesus and has not accepted Him as his/her Lord and Savior. Imagine how Jesus feels when saved folk are selfish trying to be up in Heaven by themselves? "I got my spot; you better get yours." Is that how you think? After all, Jesus has said more than once, there is joy before the angels over one sinner who repents.

Are you not willing to go the extra mile to find your lost child? Yeah, your child may have gotten on your last nerve, and you placed them on the don't call, don't talk to list. You may have written your sibling(s) off for whatever reasons. But seriously, you dislike them to the point you don't care if they are eternally damned? And you call yourself saved? You sit next to your co-workers daily and you hear them moan and groan about how bad life is. You hear them say all too often, "woe is me, and I don't have anyone to talk to or to help me." You mind your business? You decide to keep working. It's not your problem. You think to yourself "he's/she's a drama Queen! But you are saved, sanctified, and filled with the Holy Spirit? Is God's Word falling on deaf ears?

At least the father with two sons, did something you may consider a little unorthodox:

> **11** *"And he said, 'There was a man who had two sons.***12** *And the younger of them said to his father, 'Father, give me the share of property that is coming to me.' And he divided his property between them.* **13** *Not many days later, the younger son gathered all he had and took a journey into a far country, and there he squandered his property in reckless living.* **14** *And when he had spent everything, a severe famine arose in that country, and he began to be in need.* **15** *So he went and hired himself out to one of the citizens of that country, who sent him into his fields to feed pigs.* **16** *And he was longing to be fed with the pods that the pigs ate, and no one gave him anything.* **17** *But when he came to himself, he said, 'How many of my father's hired servants have more than enough bread, but I perish here with hunger!* **18** *I will arise and go to my father, and I will say to him, 'Father, I have sinned against heaven and before you.* **19** *I am no longer worthy to be called your son. Treat me as one of your hired servants.'* **20** *And he arose and came to his father. But while he was still a long way off, his father saw him and felt compassion, and ran and embraced him and kissed him.* **21** *And the*

son said to him, 'Father, I have sinned against heaven and before you. I am no longer worthy to be called your son. **22** *But the father said to his servants, 'Bring quickly the best robe, and put it on him, and put a ring on his hand, and shoes on his feet.* **23** *And bring the fattened calf and kill it, and let us eat and celebrate.* **24** *For this my son was dead, and is alive again; he was lost, and is found.' And they began to celebrate."* [Luke 15:11-24]

Before we discuss the hell that probably broke out then and would break out now between the siblings. [sort of a Cain and Abel vibe] Let's think about what Jesus is saying. This younger son, in my humble opinion, did not want to work. He wanted a glamorous life handed to him on a silver platter. He asked his father for his inheritance while his father was still alive. I know why he did not ask his mother, given the time, and a woman's role. But I know this story might have played out a little differently if mama was asked this question today. So, the father decided to honor his son's request and the son went out into the world and did his thing with prostitutes and whatever else. He lived his best life until his money ran out. Does this sound familiar? What about you? You are on top of the world, impressing people, with your luxury home(s), automobiles, vacation homes on the beach, and whatever else you can fathom. In your opinion you have it all. You have arrived, and everybody wish they could be you. This father gave his son the opportunity to experience life for himself. To roam where he wanted to and to invest or squander his great fortune…his inheritance.

You may have invested in your children's dreams. Not talking about the things, you may have purchased for them or programs, you may have put them in, like Jack and Jill, Big Brothers, & Big Sister's the Girls and Boys Club, YMCA, or YWCA etc. I am talking about handing them cash money to start a business, take ice skating lessons in pursuit of a career or Olympic gold medal in figure skating. Big Money...because you believed in his/her dream. There is a lesson in what this father did. He gave his son his inheritance. Money his son may have gotten when the father passed away. The son learned really quickly while he was out in the world, his money only went so far. It ran out. He probably had a lot of people around him who partied with him until he could no longer foot the bill. Sounds familiar? But look at what the son learned. He learned life at home wasn't so bad after all. He surmised his father treated those who worked for him better than the life he was enduring in the streets on his own. Feeding pigs and hoping to eat from the pods they ate from just wasn't his cup of tea and certainly wasn't how he was raised. But putting his big man pants on, he got a job.

The younger son realized how blessed he was to have a Father and family who loved and cared for him. He admitted he sinned against God and his family and returned home to beg his father's forgiveness and not expecting anything else from him. Jesus is letting you know he understands your youthfulness can be a burden if you are impatient and think you know everything. Young people today think because they have the internet and social media platforms, and google they can learn and know whatever they want right at their fingertips. They are not trying to learn any valuable lessons from their parent's. Just give me money for sneakers, my games, clothes, shoes, nails, and hair and begone until I need something else from you.

This father did not give his song a beat down or a bunch of I told you so's. He embraced him. He clothed him and had a big celebration. I know today, like then, his sibling(s) would have a crooked neck, jerking it back and forth in disbelief. Probably thinking the father had lost his mind. Taking this boy back when he left not having to work the fields or be responsible. You can see all hell would breakout today if it didn't break out then. Let's see how the older son, his brother, took this:

> **25** *"Now his older son was in the field, and as he came and drew near to the house, he heard music and dancing.* **26** *And he called one of the servants and asked what these things meant.* **27** *And he said to him, 'Your brother has come, and your father has killed the fattened calf, because he has received him back safe and sound.'* **28** *But he was angry and refused to go in. His father came out and entreated him,* **29** *but he answered his father, 'Look, these many years I have served you, and I never disobeyed your command, yet you never gave me a young goat, that I might celebrate with my friends.* **30** *But when this son of yours came, who has devoured your property with prostitutes, you killed the fattened calf for him!'* **31** *And he said to him, 'Son, you are always with me, and all that is mine is yours."*

This father rejoiced because his son left home spiritually dead but returned home a man spiritually alive, awakened and renewed! The older brother's, jealousy clouded his judgment and perhaps the joy he should have felt learning his brother returned alive with no scars and bruises other than his ego and pride. As an attorney, I can think of countless examples of horror stories of what family members particularly siblings do to one another when the parents die without a Will. Well to be honest some act a fool [forgive me for using the word fool] when there is a Will. People can't seem to understand people can do what they want with their money and stuff whether you like it or not. It's their stuff for them to leave it to whom they choose. I am not talking about couples who have joint wills or reciprocal wills. I am talking about people who wait for people to die as their come up in the world. It's a blessing to receive that catapults people beyond starting out with nothing. Remember a fool and his money shall soon part. [Proverbs 21:20] There are a hundred or more bible verses documenting this.

Jesus is concerned about souls. He's commanded you to go out and concern yourself with finding lost souls. Can you do that? Are you willing to go after the one sheep and bring it home to Jesus? You were lost one day, and someone took the time to help find you. *"All we like sheep have gone astray; we have turned—everyone—to his own way; and the LORD has laid on him the iniquity of us all.* [Isaiah 53:6] However, *"I have gone astray like a lost sheep; seek your servant, for I do not forget your commandments."* [Psalm 119:176] Don't be blind to Jesus Commandment. Ponder these words: *"In their case the god of this world has blinded the minds of the unbelievers, to keep them from seeing the light of the gospel of the glory of Christ, who is the image of God."* [2 Corinthians 4:4] *"My people have been lost sheep. Their shepherds have led them astray, turning them away on the mountains. From mountain to hill they have gone. They have forgotten their fold."* [Jeremiah 50:6] *"But concerning that day and hour no one knows, not even the angels of heaven. Nor the Son, but the Father only."* [Matthew 24:36]

What is your response to this? You know the devil is a deceiver and now you know if you didn't already, he has the audacity to blind unbelievers to keep them from knowing Jesus and his gift of salvation. So why walk around calling people heathens if you aren't willing to share the Good News with them? *"And Peter said to them, 'Repent and be baptized every one of you in the name of Jesus Christ for the forgiveness of your sins, and you will receive the gift of the Holy Spirit."* [Acts 2:38] *"I am the good shepherd. The good shepherd lays down his life for the sheep."* [John 10:11] *"For God so loved the world, that he gave his only Son, that whoever believes in him should not perish but have eternal life."* [John 3:16]

If you open your mouth and share the Good News with others as much as you share news, sports, weather reports, and gossip, you will help to make significant progress in reaching the lost.

Be Obedient, Share the Good News

What must you do to be saved? In its most basic terms, salvation comes from Jesus Christ, who is the only way to the Father. Jesus says, *"I am the way, the truth, and the life. No one comes to the Father except through me."* [John 14:6]

Jesus made it clear throughout His ministry that being saved is the only way to be reunited with God. The Bible says in Romans 3:23, *"for all have sinned and fall short of the glory of God."* So, those who are unsaved are spiritually separated from God — they are lost.

To be saved, one must accept the free gift of salvation Jesus offered through His death and resurrection. John 3:16, *"For God so loved the world that He gave His one and only Son, that whoever believes in Him shall not perish but have eternal life."* To accept salvation, one must trust in Jesus and choose to commit one's life to Him. Romans 10:9-10 states, *"That if you confess with your mouth, 'Jesus is Lord,' and believe in your heart that God raised Him from the dead, you will be saved. For it is with your heart that you believe and are justified, and it is with your mouth that you confess and are saved."*

When you take the step of faith and commit to following Jesus, He makes you a new creation. The Bible says in 2 Corinthians 5:17, *"Therefore, if anyone is in Christ, the new creation has come: The old has gone, the new is here."* This is true spiritual transformation. God provides you the opportunity to be found, regardless of your present, past, and future mistakes.

Being saved through Jesus is how you experience true freedom and hope. As Jesus said in John 8:36, *"So if the Son sets you free, you will be free indeed."* Salvation brings about restoration in your relationship with God and it is the key to having a meaningful life. Overall, if you are looking to be saved, the Bible provides the answers. Have you ever experienced a situation where you lost something and then found it? The lost-and-found experience can be a helpful analogy for a spiritual journey to Jesus. Trusting and believing in Jesus' gift of salvation means you will never be lost again. Instead, God found you and embraced you in His arms of love and that is where you will remain.

When you experience moments of confusion, uncertainty, and emptiness, it can feel like you are lost without direction or purpose. Your mind races to find a way out and you're desperate for someone to turn to. You may feel no matter how hard you try, there is no way forward. Jesus is the answer. He provides lasting and true freedom when you accept Him as your Lord and Savior. When you share this Good News with your neighbors and your neighbor turns to Jesus for salvation, it is like they have been found after a long and arduous search. The assurance of being known and accepted by God grants a peace that surpasses all understanding. Jesus welcomes you with open arms and promises never to leave you alone.

The journey that leads to Jesus is filled with love, dedication, commitment, and joy. It is a journey of discovering who you are in God's eyes and how much He loves and values you. This understanding can give you strength for the days ahead and a renewed sense of purpose in your life.

The lost-and-found experience is an appropriate analogy to your spiritual journey to Jesus. He is the answer to all your lost-and-found moments, providing you with unlimited freedom, acceptance, and purpose. When you surrender your life to Jesus and accept his free gift of salvation, your life will never be the same. He meets you in your moments of brokenness and sadness, consoling you and filling you with peace and grace. He frees you from the bondage of sin and provides you with ultimate acceptance and love. He walks with you, no matter what—even when you have gone astray.

Jesus gives you a deep, meaningful purpose. When you accepted Jesus as your Lord and Savior, you became part of the family of God, and faith provides you with a path for living an abundant and meaningful life. No matter where you are or how far you've gone, Jesus is there, beckoning you back to the safety of His arms. He will never abandon you, no matter what. Take courage today and accept Jesus' offer of unconditional love, acceptance, and purpose. Through Him, you will find true freedom and you will never be lost again.

Salvation Is YOURS!
GOODBYE TOILET STOOL LIFE

Pipes and plumbing systems are working perfectly.
"No Longer Out Of Order"

EPILOGUE

Jesus Has The Final Say

"You have been with me from the beginning"

The Vine and the Branches: The Relationship of Believers to Christ

15 "I am the true vine, and my Father is the gardener.[2] He cuts off every branch in me that bears no fruit, while every branch that does bear fruit, he prunes so that it will be even more fruitful. [3] You are already clean because of the word I have spoken to you. [4] Remain in me, as I also remain in you. No branch can bear fruit by itself; it must remain in the vine. Neither can you bear fruit unless you remain in me.

[5] "I am the vine; you are the branches. If you remain in me and I in you, you will bear much fruit; apart from me you can do nothing. [6] If you do not remain in me, you are like a branch that is thrown away and withers; such

branches are picked up, thrown into the fire, and burned.[7] If you remain in me and my words remain in you, ask whatever you wish, and it will be done for you. [8] This is to my Father's glory, that you bear much fruit, showing yourselves to be my disciples.

[9] "As the Father has loved me, so have I loved you. Now remain in my love. 10 If you keep my commands, you will remain in my love, just as I have kept my Father's commands and remain in his love. 11 I have told you this so that my joy may be in you and that your joy may be complete.

Love one Another

[12] My command is this: Love each other as I have loved you. [13] Greater love has no one than this: to lay down one's life for one's friends. [14] You are my friends if you do what I command. [15] I no longer call you servants, because a servant does not know his master's business. Instead, I have called you friends, for everything that I learned from my Father I have made known to you. [16] You did not choose me, but I chose you and appointed you so that you might go and bear fruit—fruit that will last—and so that whatever you ask in my name the Father will give you. [17] This is my command: Love each other.

The World Hates Christ's Disciples

[18] "If the world hates you, keep in mind that it hated me first. [19] If you belonged to the world, it would love you as its own. As it is, you do not belong to the world, but I have chosen you out of the world. That is why the world hates you. [20] Remember what I told you: 'A servant is not greater than his master.' If they persecuted me, they will persecute you also. If they obeyed my teaching, they will obey yours also. [21] They will treat you this way because of my name, for they do not know the one who sent me. [22] If I had not come and spoken to them, they would not be guilty of sin; but now they have no excuse for their sin. [23] Whoever hates me hates my Father as well. [24] If I had not done among them the works no one else did, they would not be guilty of sin. As it is, they have seen, and yet they have hated both me and my Father. [25] But this is to fulfill what is written in their Law: 'They hated me without reason.

The Spirit and the Witness

[26] "When the Advocate comes, whom I will send to you from the Father—the Spirit of truth who goes out from the Father—he will testify about me. [27] And you also must testify, for you have been with me from the beginning."

Made in the USA
Monee, IL
23 June 2024

60063284R00174